MW01711296

oinlac

pherd

Nov. 10, 2018

Dear Deacon Stan, Darlene
& Family,

Peace & good tidings!
I humbly implore Christs'
priestly blessings &
heavenly favours to
both of you & to your
entire household.

Prayerfully,
Fr. Nilo Macapinlac

Nilo Macapinlac

The Voice Of The Good Shepherd

"Speak Lord, Your Servant Is Listening"

Blessed Hope Publishing

Imprint

Cover image: www.ingimage.com

Publisher:
Blessed Hope Publishing
is a trademark of
International Book Market Service Ltd., member of OmniScriptum Publishing Group
17 Meldrum Street, Beau Bassin 71504, Mauritius

Printed at: see last page
ISBN: 978-620-2-47782-6

In the Midst Of The World's Noise Attune To The Shepherd's Voice

By Reverend Nilo Belvis Macapinlac, pastor

A pastoral message of encouragement for God's flock, to attune to the Word of God despite of the busy and noisy world where we live in. Words both of inspirations and challenges that lead us to hope and to have faith to the One who holds our bright future and above all to the One who gives us life eternal,

Jesus Christ, the Incarnate Word.

Foreword

"If today you hear God's voice, harden not your hearts." *(Hebrews 3:15)* In the Old Testament God spoke through the prophets but in the fullness of time, God spoke through His Incarnate Word, Jesus Christ, His Only Begotten Son. *(Heb. 1:1ff)*

At the River Jordan and Mt. Tabor, the heavens opened and the voice of the Eternal Father was heard: "***This is my beloved Son in whom I am well pleased, listen to Him."*** *(Lk 9:35/3:22, Mk. 9:7/Mt. 3;17)*. When we listen to Jesus we are directly listening to the Eternal Father.

God the Father Himself revealing to us His Only Begotten Son, Jesus. Therefore, when we obey the commands of Jesus to love one another, we are following the Commandments of God, we in turn obeying the Father.

King David in Psalm 23, he declared: ***"The Lord is my Shepherd there's nothing I shall want"***. As the greatest king of Israel, he prophesied the coming of the Messiah who will be the Shepherd of Israel, who will lay down His life as a ransom for many.

Moreover, John the Baptist identified Him as well as the "Lamb of God" who will take away the sins of His people. This Good Shepherd who willingly and passionately giving up Himself for our sake and for our salvation is no other than Jesus the Christ. He was the fulfillment of all the prophesies of all the prophets.

Jesus Himself claimed, ***"I am the Good Shepherd." "The Good Shepherd lays down his life for his sheep."*** (John 10:14) ***"I know my sheep and my sheep know Me." "My sheep listen to my voice, I know them and they follow Me"*** (John 10:27)

In today's busy and noisy secular and materialistic world, there are many voices and some people are confused whose voice they will listen to. It seemed likened to Adam and Eve in the Book of Genesis, they listened to the voice of God who walked with them at the garden but they both were deceived by another voice.

Not only the voice of their selfish and inner cravings, the desires of the flesh, but they listened to the voice of the Devil, the father of lies and prince of darkness. Thus, after listening to the diabolical serpent and disobeyed God, sin has entered their souls and the consequence of sin was death.

The only remedy was the coming of the Only Begotten Son, Jesus into our world who Himself was lifted up on the tree of the Cross who became the fruit of our salvation. At His Altar Table of the Eucharist, He Himself is our food for eternal life.

He became our victor-king who conquered sin and death through His Cross and resurrection, the first fruit of those who have fallen asleep. ***"For God so loved the world that He gave us His Only Begotten Son that whoever believes in Him may not perish but have eternal life".*** (John 3:16).

In this valley of tears, we the poor banished children of Adam and Eve, let us fix our gaze upon the Son of God, Jesus Christ who alone has the word of everlasting life. This gift is gratuitously bestowed upon us by the Eternal Word Incarnate, Jesus.

Striving to be His faithful disciples, let us listen to Him and put into practice His words and follow Him who is our Good Shepherd. He is a guarantee that we will not walk astray nor lost along the way to the path of salvation. For ***"He is the Way, the Truth and the Life, no comes to the Father, except through Me",*** (John 14:6) says the

Lord. He was the Only One who came down from heaven and so he alone can guide us how to go there.

This booklet is the compilation of my pastoral message published on the parish bulletin which might give you encouragement to move forward in embracing the faith especially embracing God that matters most in our journey in this world. Surely, He who accompanies us to our ultimate destiny, which is heaven through His Son, the Good Shepherd.

This could challenge you also since His desire, is for us to grow and prosper in our personal relationship with Him. I hope and pray that you may hear His voice through His Word extracted in my writings that one day after listening to Him, you may live the Word of God and have the courage to share and to witness to His Gospel.

St. Thomas Aquinas, the "Angelic Doctor of the Church" once said: "Nemo dat quod non habit" which means "You cannot give what you do not have."

May the Lord be with you always and may His Word be a lamp to your feet and a light unto your path. May the Word of God find His Sanctuary in your heart. May you bear the life of Christ in abundance through His Word and Sacraments.

Table of Contents

Message of Hope: *"Brokenness in our world needs not despair but hope for healing"*

Pope Francis exhorts us with these words: "Let the Church always be a place of mercy and hope, where everyone is welcomed, loved and forgiven." The Church is a mother and also a teacher who guides all her children to grow in love and holiness. The Church is also an institution established as the Bride of Christ whose relationship is inseparable and indissoluble, to whom the blood of the Lamb of God was poured out for the remission of the sins of the world.

However, as being comprised of frail human beings with fallen nature, she needs the Groom, Jesus Christ for her redemption. The Second Vatican Council calls the Church as the People of God and St. Paul's letter fondly calls her as the "Mystical Body of Christ."

The Body of Christ today is still wounded and broken because of the imperfections and shortcomings of her children. Not only by the faithful or ordinary followers of Christ but by some members of the clergy which we are saddened here in the Americas. Literally, she is as wounded as Christ's Body was wounded on the Cross! How do we take some steps of remedy to heal Christ's Body?

My professor in Social Justice when I was taking my degree in contemporary philosophy raised this question: "When you wake up in the morning, do you consider yourself as part of the problem or part of the solution? If you are part of the solution then you are part of the process of healing the wounds of the Body of Christ.

In the Biblical sense, the first that wounds the relationship between God and humanity was through rebellion and disobedience of the first parents, Adam and Eve. They were in paradise who walked with God. All creation and the |Creator are in harmony, with amazing beauty and in the order of grace, supernatural grace.

But, when the Devil intervened to trick the first parents and followed the dictate of unclean spirits, they no longer listened to the voice of God. They succumb to temptation and they ate the fruit of the tree of knowledge of good and evil.

In fact, they listened to the voice of their ego, of their selfish cravings and obeyed the voice of the ancient diabolical serpent, Satan, the prince of lies and darkness. Chaos, disorder, division and discord continue to prevail in their lives and in the world they live in and in our world today. Original sin creep in into our human condition and death captured us.

Adam blamed Eve and conjugal relationship begins to torn apart. Eve blamed the serpent which brought chaos to nature and God's creation. The consequences of original sin brought forth the poison of the soul and sickness leads to death. "All have sinned and are deprived of the glory of God!" Rom. 3:20. "But thanks be to Jesus Christ whose gift is eternal life for those who believe in Him.

If the Fall of Adam and Eve has consequences that shuts paradise for us, our immortality turns into mortality, that death entered our soul, and the dynamism of original sin contaminates the entire human race. How God can resolve this prevailing problem since eating the forbidden fruit of the tree that these chaos, death and eternal damnation had entered our lives and our world?

The key answer is Jesus Christ who is the medicine and balm of healing Himself. He who is the fruit of the tree, of that immortal tree of the Cross becomes the remedy for our salvation and eternal life which He wanted to perpetuate this everlasting memory.

At the Last Supper during the institution of the Holy Eucharist, he said: "Do this in memory of Me." What a spiritual paradox that His own very body was wounded and His own glorified body in the Eucharist is the remedy and healing. Not only that He became the source of eternal salvation. "He who eats this bread and drink this blood has eternal life! The Sacraments are instituted by Christ Himself to pour out sanctifying grace for our sake and for our salvation.

In the midst of the brokenness of the heart wounded by sin, Christ reconcile us to the Father through His Cross, and poured out this immense grace of healing in the Sacrament of Confession or Reconciliation. Do we apply this redeeming grace of God revealed by Jesus to us in this Sacrament? How often do you come to apply this grace in your life?

If you come to see your doctor in a regular basis, do you apply this also in your spiritual growth to holiness? Our blood test results can be compared to the examination of our conscience, there through our moral conscience God speaks, reminding us to do good and avoid evil. Our clean and clear conscience aid us to seek God and made Him center of our lives and the ultimate priority.

In the midst of our vulnerability to sickness and dreaded diseases, Christ Himself is our Divine physician. He caress our soul with the oil of healing which probably Adam and Eve long at the Garden of Eden but they cannot find any herb for medicine. If you felt that you are terribly sick or someone in your family almost dying, do you request that this sacrament would be applied to them?

In the midst of spiritual hunger and being famished in the desert, in the land of slavery to sin, vices and drowning to addiction and impurities, do we reconcile to God and nourish ourselves with the Bread of Life, the Holy Eucharist? Do we go to Church every Sunday? How committed are you to Christ? Can you say that your commitment to Christ is proportionate to the solidity of your faith?

As we already experienced conflict deep within us, how do we find remedy? Likewise in the midst of division, discord and conflict, how do we move forward? Let us re-discover God's balm of healing through His unconditional love unfold in the Sacraments of the Church. Do we allow ourselves to be the channel of God's grace and blessings?

We can be God instruments of peace and order in our world today. Do we comfort Christ in the depressed and poor brothers and sisters of ours? In the midst of violence do we pray for our persecutors, do we bless those who cursed us and further more Christ asked of us to love our enemies?

One of my friends email this article which probably we can make it as a tool for our reflection this month, entitles: "The Lord's Clinic".

I went to the Lord's clinic to have my routine check-up and I confirmed that I was ill. When Jesus took my blood pressure, He saw I was low in compassion and tenderness, above all with patience. When He read my body temperature, the thermometer registered 40 degrees of useless anxiety. He ran an electrocardiogram and found that I need several "love bypasses" since my arteries were blocked with loneliness, rejection and could not provide for an empty heart.

I went to orthopedics because I could not walk by my brother's side and I could not hug some of my friends since I fractured myself when tripping with envy and jealousy. He is also a great opthalmologist which he found out I was short sighted, since I could not see beyond the short comings of my brothers and sisters.

When I complained about deafness, the diagnostic was that I had stopped listening to the voice of the Lord, I had stopped attuning to the voice of Jesus who spoke to me on a daily basis in my interior life which led to the deterioration of my spiritual life, a life of prayer.

For all of that, Jesus gave me a free consultation at confession. Thanks to his gentleness and compassion. And so, I humbly pledge that once I leave this clinic, I only take the natural remedies he prescribed through His words of wisdom and truth:

Every morning, take a full glass of gratitude and of sense of appreciation. When getting to work, take one spoon of peace and meekness. Every hour, take one pill of patience, one cup of friendship and one table spoon of humility.

When getting home, take one dose of loving tender care. When getting to bed, count your blessings and take two caplets of clear conscience. Do not give in into sadness or desperation for what you are going through today. God knows how you feel because He became human in Jesus Christ. He embrace you dearly close to His Sacred Heart.

God's purpose for you is simply perfect. He wants to show you things that only you can understand by living what you are living and by being in the place where you are now.

May God grant you for every storm, a rainbow, for every tear, a smile, for every care, a promise. A blessing in each trial and for every problem life sends---a loyal and faithful friend to share! For every sigh, a sweet song and an answer to each prayer, let God carry you for there is no problem too big that our God cannot solve.

I would like to invite again some people whom I meet at coffee shops, in stores and other functions and parties or house blessing who are interested of becoming Catholic.

Please don't hesitate to call our parish church and connect with one of our staff or to our RCIA Coordinator. Our door is open wide for you. You will be embraced by our parish community and above all by our Almighty Lord, Father, Son and Holy Spirit.

I humbly entrust you to God's loving embrace....I implore His priestly blessings to you and to all your loved ones.

Time is a Gift: *"Christian Stewardship values time as gold above all when God walks with His people in the richness of His Mercy on the Extraordinary Jubilee Year."*

New year has come, time is reckoning. Our God who is rich in mercy, walks with us shaping our history and destiny. In Latin, often times it is well quoted: **"Tempus fugit"** which means "time flies". Time is a gift from the Lord, let us not waste time but rather value it in a productive way.

Let this Extraordinary Jubilee Year of Mercy not pass without benefiting from its enormous grace and spiritual blessings to be applied both for the living and the deceased.

St. Paul would remind us of the urgency of the gospel proclamation: "NOW is the time of salvation. Now is the accepted time!" God is transcendent yet palpable to our human experience, who is Immanuel (God with us) if we have faith in His Only Begotten Son, Jesus. It transcends space and time and reaches to the infinite spheres of eternity.

The merits of Christ's passion and death on the Cross and His glorious resurrection is being applied to our sanctification and salvation. Christ the Lord said: "No one comes to the Father except through Me." Christ mercy reaches out to us spontaneously and over flowingly!

He is the vehicle that could assure us that we can reach heaven with certainty and no doubt at all. Let us turn to the Most Sacred Heart of Jesus, the oasis of mercy in season and out of season.

"Merciful Like the Father" is the theme of this Jubilee Year that comes from the gospel according to Luke 6:36. Let us humble ourselves before the Lord and in the midst of the misery of life and our human weakness, let us acknowledge the need of His mercy, our need of God the Father of mercies.

Let us encounter His merciful love, healing, forgiveness and unfathomable mercy in the Sacrament of Penance. I highly encourage you my dear friends to begin your new year with the Sacrament of Mercy, the Sacrament of Penance or Reconciliation.

How can we extend the mercy of God if we are not compassionate enough to allow God's merciful forgiveness in our lives? Remember that through Baptism we are called to be Christ's Ambassadors of reconciliation. Please don't forget to forgive yourselves, then we can move to forgive others.

St. Francis of Assisi once said: "It is in pardoning that we are pardoned." Inspired by the very prayer of Jesus: "For give us our sins as we forgive those who sinned against us."

The central message of the Pontificate of Pope Francis is truly Divine Mercy and pardon, which he convoked an extraordinary jubilee year to be called the Holy Year of Mercy.

Saying he has "thought often about how the church can make more evident its mission of being a witness of mercy," the pope announced the new jubilee year during a Lenten penitential service in St. Peter's Basilica. *"I am convinced that the whole church -- that has much need to receive mercy because we are sinners — will find in this jubilee the joy to rediscover and render fruitful the mercy of God, with which we are all called to give consolation to every man and woman of our time,"*

Moreover, Pope Francis said in announcing the year. *"Let us not forget that God pardons and God pardons always," the pope continued. "Let us never tire of asking for forgiveness."We entrust it as of now to the Mother of Mercy, because she looks to us with her gaze and watches over our way,"*

His Holiness Pope Francis said. "Our penitential way, our way of open hearts, during a year to receive the indulgence of God, to receive the mercy of God." The pope also said he wants the church to live the upcoming holy year "in the light" of Jesus' words in the Gospel of Luke: ***"Be merciful, just as your Father is merciful."***

A jubilee year is a special year called by the church to receive blessing and pardon from God and remission of sins. The Catholic church has called jubilee years every 25 or 50 years since the year 1300 and has also called special jubilee years from time to time, known as extraordinary jubilee years.

The last jubilee year was held in 2000 during the papacy of Pope John Paul II and was known as "the Great Jubilee." The last extraordinary jubilee year was held in 1983 to celebrate 1,950 years since the death and resurrection of Jesus. Pope Francis said that the new jubilee would begin on this year's Catholic feast of the Immaculate Conception, celebrated Dec. 8. It will close on Nov. 20, 2016, the day celebrated that year as the feast of Christ the King.

Announcing the closing date, the pope added a new term to the title of Christ celebrated that day, also calling Jesus *"the living face of the mercy of the Father." "No one can be excluded from the mercy of God,"* Francis continued, repeating: *"No one can be excluded from the mercy of God!" "The church is the house that welcomes all and refuses no one,"* the pope said. *"Its doors remain wide open, so that those touched by grace can find the certainty of forgiveness."*

I would like to thank our priests in the deanery and beyond who came to minister to all the penitents, the Sisters of Merciful Jesus with their advent reflection and mission on how we can be the channel of God's mercy, the various religious organizations and staff of our Sacred Heart Parish, Wetaskiwin, and special committee on the Extraordinary Jubilee Year of Mercy for their input, collaboration and hard work that we were able to enter into the spirit of the Holy Year of Mercy.

To our school principal who prepared our entire school family to have the first time penitential service with emphasis on Divine Mercy and individual confessions, I am deeply grateful for the greater glory of God!

Kindly read our parish bulletin for some important updates on the Year of Mercy in our parish and school and in the Archdiocese at large. Let us live the mercy of God daily and exercising both the spiritual and corporal works of mercy in our school, home, office, farm, parish and wherever we are called by the Father of mercies to serve.

May the Lord enrich you with His infinite mercy and abounding love throughout this Holy Year of Mercy!

Divine Mercy: *"A gift at Christmas & at All Season, We need to live and Share"*

Christ is truly in our hearts as we live His merciful love in season and out of season. Christmas is the birth of Christ not only in the lowly manger of Bethlehem but in the manger of our hearts.

Let us celebrate this joy-filled season with sharing what we have to our least fortunate ones. Let us stand together to make our world a haven of peace and a better place to live in.

As we enter into the spirit of the Extraordinary Jubilee Year of Mercy, let us execute and live the corporal and spiritual works of mercy. Surely, what we have done to the least fortunate we have done it to Christ!

Indeed, there is joy not only in receiving gifts but above all, also in giving. St. Francis of Assisi rightly says: "It is in giving of ourselves that we receive, it is in pardoning that we are pardoned and it is in dying that we are born to eternal life." This is a basic principle in the life of every good stewards in God's house.

This season is not only a grace-filled opportunity to share what we have to the poor, the homeless, the broken-hearted, but it is the season to reflect on how we were able to receive and accept, God's gift of salvation: JESUS CHRIST.

When you have a personal relationship with the Lord, are you ready to witness His love and mercy to others? The answer is Yes! By Baptism we are called to be evangelizers and in Confirmation, we are sealed by the gifts of the Holy Spirit to be His witnesses of His love and mercy in our world today.

These religious pamphlets and articles are which the parish Christmas gifts for you to read and ponder God's mercy and to grow in charity.

May you prosper and you may advance in the love of God and neighbour not only in this Jubilee Year of Mercy but throughout your lives. Being good stewards of time, talent and treasures we are called to be good evangelizers and witnesses of Christ.

"For God so loved the world that He gave us His Only Begotten Son that whoever believes in Him may not perish or die but have an everlasting life." John 3:16.

I humbly invoke Christ priestly blessings upon you and upon members of your entire family in the name of the + Father and of the Son and of the Holy Spirit, Amen. A very Merry Christmas and a New Year filled with grace and heavenly blessings to all of you!

The Resurrection of Christ: *"The Foundation of our Hope for Eternal life"*

Let us join the entire Christian world to celebrate with joy our fresh new day, the day of Christ's victory, the Easter Resurrection. Easter is the highest feast of the Church. St. Paul to the Gentiles reminds us that if Christ is not resurrected from the dead, then our preaching and proclamation of the Gospel is futile and in vain.

Christ is indeed truly resurrected from the dead, victorious and ever glorious, alive forever more! Death had been swallowed up to victory. The great apostle Paul reminded his faith community as he exclaimed with joyful proclamation: "O death where is your victory, O death where is your sting, now that Jesus has been resurrected from the dead?!"

The victory of Christ is the victory of all believers. This is the fruit of the magnitude of God's love for us who never spared to sacrifice His Only Begotten Son, Jesus that ***whoever believes in Him may not perish but have an everlasting life.*** (cf. John 3:16). The LOVE crucified will never die! Love indeed is eternal.

Alleluiah is our song, sure hope is our banner, Christ is our Victor-King! Rejoice all you, Christians, the tomb is empty. Satan, sin and death had been conquered, darkness had been banished.

Let the light of Christ in you be kept burning brightly for we are truly as such, sons and daughters of the Light. The Risen Christ confirms: "You are the light of the world." Let no one walk alone, let us us march together on the way to our heaven where Christ reigns.

Let us share the light of Christ to others through our major pastoral priorities here in our Sacred Heart Parish, Wetaskiwin. Carry the light of Christ in our mission to evangelize, increase the light, let it burn brightly through our faith formation and let it ignite its flame in fostering the culture of vocations at home, school and in our parish and in the entire strata of our society today.

Christ the Lamb of God, once slain but dies no more! Let us walk the talk and apply the fruits of His redeeming love to our lives and share it to others especially those who are in dire need of His love, compassion and mercy. Christ is our Divine Mercy to whom I commend those who are dying and those who died unprepared and without any spiritual preparation.

Life is too short, eternity is without end. Regret comes last and so let us live the Christian life worthy of our calling for the day is coming like the thief and we don't know when it comes. Let us allow ourselves to be envelope by God's love and be anointed by His Divine Mercy.

Next Sunday is the Divine Mercy Sunday, I simply invite you to pray the Chaplet of the Divine Mercy. Let us put into action the mercy of the Lord. We have to live His compassion through the spiritual and corporal works of mercy.

I encourage you all to practice our faith that produces God's mercy. St. Augustine reminds us that Mercy is the greatest of all attributes of the Lord for without it we were not be brought to salvation through His Cross.

Let us strengthen our confidence and trust in Him as the secretary apostle of Divine Mercy, St. Faustina Kowaslka attests:" JESU UFAM TOBIE" a Polish phrase which means JESUS I TRUST IN YOU.

Total trust even exposes all secrets to the beloved and so at the tribunal of justice and mercy, Christ awaits all of us. The Sacrament of Confession is the pre-requisite to celebrate this Divine Mercy Sunday.

We had already the avenues: Day of Confession, Penitential Service and Confessions and Confessions every before Mass. Jesus revealed its deepest secret, we may become anew like infant newly baptize before our loving Creator. Please don't waste this God -given privilege and providence. Apply now the merits of His merciful passion and His passion for mercy for your souls.

The Holy Gospel that the Liturgy will present to us this coming second Sunday of Easter, is one of the most well known, discussed, and appreciated – the meeting of the Risen Lord with St Thomas.

The Fathers of the Church have given us numerous insights into this Gospel text. Likewise, it is has proven the inspiration to the numerous artists who have physically represented the events of this Gospel in order to give us a clear idea of what happened, 'eight days after' the first apparition of the Risen One, to the disciples congregated in the cenacle.

Jesus' response to Thomas, after he recognised Him as ***'My Lord and my God'***, has a mysterious fascination that must relate not so much to the disciples – those who *'have seen'* – but rather to those, like us, who were added to their number afterwards. ***'You have come to believe because you have seen me. Blessed are those who have not seen and have believed.'***(Jn 20:29)

The attention that these words evoke seams yet more paradoxical if we remember that the Lord had proposed, to the same author of the Gospel, what can be justly referred to as the Christian method, ***'come and see'***(Jn 1:39).

How can we possibly reconcile these two phrases by Jesus that form the ideal setting for the whole of the fourth Gospel? Perhaps, in the end, the Lord decided to change His method? What do the words *'have not seen'* really mean?

The timely recollection of the 'eight days after,' which is the Sunday after the Resurrection, permits us to tie our reflection to one of the most significant Eucharistic hymns composed by another Thomas, St Thomas Aquinas, the patron of our Catholic school division.

In the *Adore Te Devote*, which refers to the Eucharist, we read: *'Sight, touch, taste are all deceived in their judgement of you. But hearing suffices firmly to believe'.*

Combining these words with the Divine Mercy Sunday's Gospel we can justly affirm that the experience *'to see'* was not denied to us, but it is in contrast with the Apostle Thomas' physical experience, who was able to put his own finger into the sacred wounds in Christ's hands and side, while we can only comprehend it in the faith which is guarded and transmitted by the Church, our Mother and Teacher.

That which we *'have not seen'* is therefore the glorious Body of the Risen One. However, today we have the ability to *'listen'* to the Word of God and the Magisterium of the Church and so we can *'see'* the real Body of Christ which is the Eucharist.

We can *'see'* His Mystical Body which is the Church. We can *'see'* Him in our lives and in the lives of our many brothers who, after meeting the Lord in a real but mysterious way, are united to Him in His Spirit!

Like Thomas, Christ calls us to fill the holes left by the instruments of the passion in His Body with our own hands so that our lives and the verbal witness that we give proclaim His Resurrection.

Our senses thus, could betray us, but we know that we have met the Risen One and we have recognised Him! The certain hope that Peter, who betrayed the Lord three times for fear of death, proclaims to us with the words, *'rejoice with an indescribable and glorious joy'* (1 Peter 1:8), become fully comprehensible because blessed are they that *'have not seen'* the Risen Lord, but seeing the joy of His disciples *'have believed'* in Him!

May the Resurrected Christ smile upon you this Octave of Easter and lift you up in all your struggles and difficulties in life. Believe Him, Trust in Him, Love Him. For truly He will enrich you with heavenly blessings! In the Most Sacred Heart of Jesus wounded out of love for us, let us place our confidence in Him. Amen

The Son of Man & The Son of God: *"True Model for Us to Follow on Our 40 Days Journey at Lent."*

Our journey of faith for 40 days this Lenten season is crucial in our spiritual growth as God's people here in Wetaskiwin. Let us observe it and not to be stocked up in ritualistic manner but in the spirit of love and freedom. It should be rooted in our love for the Lord and the grace bounds back to us in a manifold way.

Let God's grace illumine our souls through confession knowing that sin darkens the image of God in us and even disfiguring it. Thanks for your generous hearts in responding positively to the day of confession and of course to our forthcoming penitential service on March 24 at 7pm. In my Ignatian retreat for only twelve days, we begin with confession and nourished by the Eucharist and the Word of God.

Expect distractions and temptations that they may led you to give up but don't surrender. Temptation is not a sin but to give -in is the down fall of our soul. Remember God counts how much we struggle. Retreat to the wilderness and invite God to accompany you, be attuned to the prompting of the Holy Spirit.

Though God respects our human freedom but He is never tired of reaching out to us for our sakes and for our redemption. For no one can save himself or herself, we totally rely on God's loving act of salvation and we need to cooperate.

We cannot reap the harvest unless we toil and do our portion in hard work. The trees and shrubs will not sprout unless there is water, moisture, soil, minerals and the sunlight. We need to wait and patience is the key until the time of harvest. In the springtime of your spiritual life you will bloom and be filled with joy that comes directly from God. You will never regret.

The first Sunday of Lent lead us directly to the wilderness of our spiritual life and we need to acknowledge our human weakness and vulnerability. We need God and His necessary graces for us to persevere. Jesus is our model and guide, let us turn to Him in silent prayer.

"The Spirit drove Jesus out into the wilderness and he remained there for forty days, and was tempted by Satan" (Mk 1:12-13). Having introduced the season of Lent here in our Sacred Heart Parish with the imposition of ashes, the Church points out the path for us to journey along. She also tells us the nature of this journey and how we might go about following it.

The Gospel reading shows us how the journey of Lent consists in letting ourselves be led into the desert, allowing ourselves to remain there for forty days, and challenging ourselves to face the temptations of Satan.

It is likened to the Exodus of Israel towards the Promised Land; it is the exodus of humanity with each of us journeying as pilgrims towards heaven. We don't look forward to this journey for its own sake, but we are led along it by Another.

The journey is signposted by our combat with the temptation of Satan and - with all that implies in terms of fatigue and suffering. It is a long journey which only our sure hope allows us to undertake with faith and courage.

The nature of this Lenten journey is revealed in the collect, the opening prayer, addressed to God, Our Father, that "we may grow in understanding of the riches hidden in Christ and by worthy conduct pursue their effect".

This Lenten journey is a "sacramental sign" of our conversion. What does this mean? "Sacramental sign" means that on this road, that is common to every person, God has preceded us and has done something for us and now He asks us to play our part. He has already fulfilled this journey of conversion for us.

The model to follow is Jesus Christ, "the Son of Man and the Son of God". "The Spirit drove Jesus out into the desert." It is Christ, true God and true Man, ***"the righteous for the sake of the unrighteous"*** (1 Pt 3:18) who has taken upon Himself our sins and by His free choice, as He was without sin and totally immune to it, has decided to also face our temptations.

St Augustine wrote: "Christ took his flesh from you and in return gave you the salvation that resides in him; he took your death for himself and gave you his life; he took the share you deserved and gave you the honour that was his. Consequently, he took your temptation and gave you his victory." (*Comm in Ps., 60*).

It is not asked of us, therefore, to make this journey simply by 'doing likewise'. There would be nothing new in that, because, whether we like it or not, our daily life is already like this with all its hard work and hopes! We are asked, in fact, to welcome what is new about Lent: the Other on this path, who is our companion, who has already journeyed on the path of the Exodus, and who has associated us, by our Baptism, with His Victory.

We are all called to stay close to Christ, giving over everything to him - our flesh, our sin, our humiliations, and our temptations - so that we can receive back so much more. He offers us His Salvation, His Life, His Glory, His Victory! Let's, therefore, give everything to the Lord in the great gift of sacramental Confession, in Eucharistic adoration and in frequent Communion, where Jesus takes our entirety and gives us His Very Self.

Let us trust everything to our "greatest friend", that God has placed at our side. Let us pray fervently for our catechumens and candidates that they may not only fully embrace the richness of our Catholic Faith but they may totally embrace God who is Father, Son and Holy Spirit who loves us first and initiated us to walk humbly in this noble vocation to love.

And so we offer all our sacrifices and hardships to the Sorrowful and Immaculate Heart of Mary, because she who is the "Gate of heaven", will distribute to humanity the merits of her Son. "Obtain for us, we pray, O Mary, that we will keep our eyes fixed on Christ so to defeat, along with Him, the temptations of Satan and thus we may enter into the victory of the Easter Resurrection and gain the gift of Eternal Life through Christ, our Lord". Amen.

May the burning love of the Most Sacred Heart of Jesus and the Immaculate Heart of His Mother enrich you with spiritual gifts and heavenly favours! God truly loves you dearly!

Jesus, The Lamb of God: "Wounded on the Cross, Our Greatest Healer"

The Most Sacred Heart of the Good Shepherd, Jesus our Lord is moved with pity for those who are tormented by illness, pains and sufferings. He invites us to come closer to him as he said: "Come to Me all you who are carrying heavy burdens and I will give you rest. For my yoke is easy and my burden is light."

As we are about to celebrate the World Day Prayer for the Sick on the feast day of Our Lady of Lourdes, February 11, 2015, Healing Masses will be celebrated along with the anointing of the Sick at Sacred Heart Parish at 9:00 a.m. and at Wetaskiwin Hospital at 11:00 a.m. that very day.

Everyone is welcome to experience the healing power of our God. Let us come and worship Him with unwavering faith and humble adoration. The Gospel reminds us as Jesus said: "Your faith heals you!"

Truly, without faith in God, we cannot please Him. Let us ask the Lord that day to increase our faith in Him. To let our faith be contagious to heal others who are broken hearted and infirmed. We cannot give what we do not have, St. Thomas Aquinas said.

And so, let us ask the Lord to enrich us with faith that could lead us to our sanctification and lead others to their salvation too. May Our Lady of Lourdes, Health of the Sick be with us in this time of need. She, whom the Archangel Gabriel proclaimed as "full of Grace" will dispense necessary graces for us to come closer to the Lord and experience God's healing love and mercy. She is our mother who loves and cares for us!

Let us learn how important is the sacrament of Holy Anointing for the Sick through the great teaching of the Catholic Church, the great custodian of the faith that comes directly from Jesus Christ, the Lord.

The Church believes and confesses that among the seven sacraments there is one especially intended to strengthen those who are being tried by illness**, the Anointing of the Sick:** (The Catechism of the Catholic Church 1511).

This sacred anointing of the sick was instituted by Christ our Lord as a true and proper sacrament of the New Testament. It is alluded to indeed by Mark, but is recommended to the faithful and promulgated by James the apostle and brother of the Lord.

From ancient times in the liturgical traditions of both East and West, we have testimonies to the practice of anointing of the sick with blessed oil. Over the centuries the Anointing of the Sick was conferred more and more exclusively on those at the point of death. Because of this it received the name "Extreme Unction." Notwithstanding this evolution the liturgy has never failed to beg the Lord that the sick person may recover his health if it would be conducive to his salvation.[126] (The Catechism of the Catholic Church 1512)

The Apostolic Constitution "*Sacram unctionem infirmorum*", following upon the Second Vatican Council,established that henceforth, in the Roman Rite, the following be observed:

The sacrament of Anointing of the Sick is given to those who are seriously ill by anointing them on the forehead and hands with duly blessed oil - pressed from olives or from other plants - saying, only once: "Through this holy anointing may the Lord in his love and mercy help you with the grace of the Holy Spirit. May the Lord who frees you from sin save you and raise you up." (The Catechism of the Catholic Church 1513)

My dear people of God, please be mindful of the spiritual needs of your elderly and the sick members of your family. Let us apply this tremendous heavenly blessings of our God. How many people die every day without spiritual preparation. In fact, we don't know when we will depart this temporary world of ours. Blessed are those who are sick who were chosen by the Lord to participate in His redemptive sufferings for they have almost a glimpse when the time to see Him face to face.

Kindly contact me at my emergency mobile phone printed on our bulletin and website when someone whether member of your family or your friend who is sick in serious condition, for me to come or visit that loved one. Prepare the person to have a good disposition to receive the Sacrament of reconciliation/Confession, the Anointing of the Sick and the Holy Viaticum or Holy Communion for the Sick on that day of Divine appointment.

This is one way to avoid panic and in the midst of busy life, you were able to prioritize the spiritual needs of your loved ones. And so, to capsulate what we discuss about the catechesis of this sacrament, let us reflect upon its tremendous value and effects. The special grace of the sacrament of the Anointing of the Sick has as its effects:

1. the uniting of the sick person to the passion of Christ, for his own good and that of the whole Church;

2.the strengthening, peace, and courage to endure in a Christian manner the sufferings of illness or old age;

3. the forgiveness of sins, if the sick person was not able to obtain it through the sacrament of Penance;

4. the restoration of health, if it is conducive to the salvation of his soul; and finally,

5.the preparation for passing over to eternal life.

After fulfilling our Christian duties my dear friends and parishioners, by fulfilling the will of God upon our lives and the lives of others entrusted to us, we are at peace and experience already the foretaste of the joy of our salvation on earth.

What a life fully lived and rooted in the gospel stewardship, shepherding the needs of the soul, spiritual growth, holiness and immediate preparation for our particular judgement. We were able to steward here not only the material things entrusted to us, time, talent, treasures but above all we became stewards of the spiritual needs of our brothers and sisters, truly stewards of the mysteries of our ever loving God!

Till then, to the next chapter. I humbly remain and implore the richness of Christ's priestly blessings,+ in the name of the Father, and of the Son, and of the Holy Spirit. Amen

St Valentine's Feast In February: *"Feast of Human Hearts, Above All, Feast of the Divine Love"*

February is the month of love since we are celebrating Valentine's day on the 14th. It is the feast of hearts. Above all it should be centered on the love of our God which we call "agape". A divine love, the unconditional love of God that enflames or enkindles our hearts drawn from the Sacred Heart of Jesus wounded by our offenses. Terribly wounded but heals, whose love is stronger than the power of death.

February 11 is the feast also of our Lady of Lourdes, "the health of the sick". Thus, the Church celebrates the World Day Prayer for the Sick. All those with infirmities and beset by sickness will be anointed by the oil of the Sacrament of Healing at 9 am Mass at Sacred Heart Parish and at 11 am at our Hospital Chapel in Wetaskiwin.

Let us be part of healing of the wounded Body of Christ, the Church. May the love of God be the source of strength in times of weakness and balm of healing for those who are sick, and hope for the despairing.

May this month be truly focused on our love and pastoral care for our sick brothers and sisters that through our gentle care for them, may God make us His effective instruments of His healing and wholeness of life. As Christ assured us: "I have come that you may have life in abundance." Let us pray also for all our doctors, nurses, care givers, pharmacists, pastoral care volunteers, infirmarians and to all those in the medical field.

Lord Jesus, by your sacred wounds we are healed and by your death on the Cross, death is conquered, through your resurrection you have given us new hope and a transformed life, heal our brokenness and all our infirmities. Teach us to be patient in time of sickness. Grant us the grace to unite our sufferings with you. Humble us in our weakness and make us your wounded-healers.

Our Lady of Lourdes, "Salus Infirmorum, ora pro nobis." Health of the Sick, pray for us. Amen

Life is A Gift: *"Above All is the gift of Eternal Life from God bestowed Upon Us Through the Beautiful Hands of His Priests"*

New year has come and indeed time flies. Every new year we begin our year with gratitude for the gift of life, life anew in the Lord. Some of us strive to have better lives. As Christians, we believe that there is no better life than a life fully live and rooted in Christ.

Some of us aspire to grow more with a deep and intimate relationship with God and so proposes to have a new year's resolution. We've just finished our advent penitential service and reconciliation which lead our hearts to burst with love and joy at Christmas, the birth of Jesus. Our hearts were purified by the mercy, loving forgiveness and the balm of healing of our Lord in the Sacrament. What a grace-filled gift to oneself and to Christ, the Lord who is our joy at Christmas.

I will lead you to reflect this new year about the piece of a story from the Titanic, a spiritual rescue and total abandonment to the will of God through the ministry of His servant, the priest. An untold story that I hope it would help you ponder how to journey with God this new year. The untold story of the Titanic's Catholic priest who went down hearing confessions

The Catholic priest gave up two spots on a lifeboat in favour of offering spiritual aid to the other victims as they all went down with the "unsinkable" vessel.

This story is being shared by Patrick B. Craine. He said that

amidst all the tales of chivalry from the Titanic disaster there is one that's not often told.

It is that of Fr. Thomas Byles, the Catholic priest who gave up two spots on a lifeboat in favour of offering spiritual aid to the other victims as they all went down with the "unsinkable" vessel.

A 42-year-old English convert, Fr. Byles was on his way to New York to offer the wedding Mass for his brother William. Reports suggest that he was reciting his breviary on the upper deck when the Titanic struck the iceberg in the twilight hours of Sunday, April 14th, 1912.

According to witnesses, as the ship went down the priest helped women and children get into the lifeboats, then heard confessions, gave absolution, and led passengers in reciting the Rosary.

Agnes McCoy, one of the survivors, says that as the great ship sank, Fr. Byles "stood on the deck with Catholics, Protestants and Jews kneeling around him."

"Father Byles was saying the rosary and praying for the repose of the souls of those about to perish," she told the New York Telegram on April 22, 1912, according to the website devoted to his memory, FatherByles.com.

In the words of the priest's friend Fr. Patrick McKenna, "He twice refused the offer of a place in a boat, saying his duty was to stay on the ship while one soul wanted his ministrations."

Nearly two weeks after the disaster, The Church Progress in St. Louis, Missouri wrote this moving tribute to the heroic priest:

In almost every line that has been written, and in every sentence that has been spoken, there stands boldly out above every other expression a picture of sublime heroism that will be copied into the pages of history. And well it may, for it is deserving of that honor.

But when it is, mention should be made of one whom pens and tongues have almost forgotten in their accounts of this awful sea tragedy. Among those who safely reached the land again no one seems to have been aware of his presence on the ship, but we may hope that many who meet him in a blissful eternity will praise God, that Father Thomas Byles was there to administer absolution unto them.

I hope and pray that this new year be a time of safe voyage, a voyage of friendship with God that lead us to a right direction. A new year full of hope and knowing that God is with us, with His grace we can accomplish many things, fulfilling His holy will as we strive daily to conform to His Holy Will. As we pray, "May God's will be done on earth as it is in heaven and may your Kingdom come!" Amen

"Our Human Hearts, Let It Be A New Manger this Christmas"

Christmas is truly in our hearts when we enthroned our Lord Jesus Christ as our personal Lord and King. He reigns in a new manger, a heart full of love, forgiveness, compassion, kindness, patience, mercy, understanding and goodness. Above all a heart which is the sanctuary of faith in God for without faith we cannot please the Lord. Faith is leading us to the world that is full of joy, peace and hope and its vehicle for us to arrive there is charity, love in action, for God is love, "Deus Caritas Est."

"Indeed, for God so loved the world that He gave us His Only Begotten Son, that whoever believes in HIM may not perish but have an everlasting life." (John 3:16). JESUS CHRIST who is eternal life is truly the greatest gift of the Almighty Father to all of us, His children who believe in HIM.

Knowing that God is love and born at Christmas, how do we live the spirit of Christmas in season and out of season? Every day is Christmas, let Christ be the Lord who reign in every beat of our hearts.

Let us live His gospel of truth and love. Let us live and practice our faith. Let us radiate the light of his love even to the unlovable. Let us bring the fragrance of his holiness and charity to the poor and the lowly. Christ the Lord was born in the humble stable of Bethlehem. Let us walk humbly configuring ourselves like Him who is the perfect image of the God whom we cannot see. To live this way is Christ and truly everyday is Christmas!

Jesus our Lord is the greatest gift of the Heavenly Father, let us be grateful for the many blessings that the Lord God has bestowed upon us. Let us thank God everyday in both small and big things that are good that we receive from the Lord.

Let us carry the light of our faith and become the beacon of hope for others. Let us love one another the way the Sacred Heart of Jesus loves us, truly our praise to God manifests not only in our lips but in our deeds. As the psalmist put this way: "From the rising of the sun to its setting may the name of the Lord be praised!"

Christ our Lord was born in Bethlehem and there was no bed, no inn for HIM and it was cold winter. Do you have a special place for JESUS in your heart? We have a special place in the mansion of the Almighty Father that Jesus has prepared for us. Above all, though Christ's heart was wounded by a lance, you and I has a special place in that wounded heart because we accepted, received and loved Him.

Bethlehem means "house of bread" where 2000 years ago the "Living Bread has come down from heaven" (John 6) was born there. Jesus Christ our Bread of Life invites us to dine with Him and partake Him at the table of His Body and Blood in the Eucharist. Will you come and receive HIM? This could be your excellent way of exchanging gifts.

A Holy Communion, that Christ whom you have received is in you and HE in you. Truly Christ is born in your spiritual and interior life! What a holy exchange and profound gift of Communion! "He who eats this Bread will live forever and I will raise him up on the last day."

You may share yourself as a volunteer as Christ offered Himself on the Cross for our salvation, and you may give some of your time, talents and treasures to Christ as your gift through our Sacred Heart Parish that could be part of your everlasting memory and perpetual legacy, your gift to the Lord God Almighty.

Give yourself as well the most special gift, who is Jesus Christ in our Mass, not only this day of his birthday, Christmas, but every Sunday and as frequent as you could. This is the Christmas secret hidden in the mystery of the Sacrament of the Holy Eucharist.

You will never regret at the end, you had the greatest gift of all. He is the one who is our beginning and He Himself is our end. From Him we came and unto Him we shall return, Christ the Alpha and the Omega and in Him is all in all, the greatest gift of all!

I cordially impart my prayerful best wishes of "A Very Merry "ChristMass" and a New Year filled with God's love and the abundance of His blessings to you and to your loved ones"!

Blessed Virgin Mary: *"Our Mother, Advent Model for Us to Imitate Her Patient Waiting for the Coming of Our Divine Messiah"*

Thank you for responding to your spiritual needs and above all your profound encounter with the merciful love and forgiveness of the Sacred Heart of Jesus through our penitential service and reconciliation night. God's mercy is indeed a balm of healing through the Sacrament!

We are grateful to our deacon Leo Farley who preached and to all the priests within the Camrose Deanery who made themselves available and to make this spiritual encounter with God made possible in our parish. This is one of the best spiritual preparations in embracing the season of Advent and Christmas.

Advent begins the new liturgical year of the Church. It is a season of grace and patient waiting or anticipation for the coming of Christ into the world. May I lead you into an advent reflection at this time and let us invite the Blessed Virgin Mary, the mother of our Lord to be our guide and outstanding model in approaching the seasons of Advent and Christmas.

This month of December we are celebrating two Marian feasts namely: December 8 -Feast of the Immaculate Conception which is the conception of the Blessed Virgin Mary in the womb of her mother, St. Anne. A conception defined as a dogma of faith which states "that the Blessed Virgin Mary was conceived without any single stain of sin or without original sin in the first moment of conception, a Divine privilege that God the Almighty has granted."

Secondly, we commemorate the feast of Our Lady of Guadalupe who appeared to San Juan Diego in the Hill of Tepeyac, Mexico and we celebrate it on December 12. So, let us journey with the Blessed Virgin Mary to whom God's favour finds rest.

As the Archangel saluted her: "Hail full of grace, the Lord is with you!" And who is to be hailed, I knew God alone. But God's messenger, archangel Gabriel has brought God's greeting and message to her to be the mother of our beloved Lord. What a profound reverence, trust and respect that comes not only from an angel but above all from God Himself. God firstly initiated such profound trust and respect to our humanity exemplified in the person of our Lady.

How do we live then the season of advent? Do you have time? Is your heart ready? Mary's heart ponders the mystery of God's love, her immaculate heart became the treasury of wisdom and God's grace. Because she has the purity of heart, a beatitude that leads us to see God and God's plan became clear for her.

The Blessed Virgin's calling from God became loud and clear since she utilizes the gift of time so wisely. She has time to pray in deepening her friendship with God, what a spirituality!. She became so familiar with her "Torah" the law of God rooted in the spirit of love. Her vocation is to love and she placed God at the center of her life.

She accepted wholeheartedly her vocation to be the mother of our Lord and Saviour, Jesus Christ, the Eternal Word of the Father incarnated in her womb by the Holy Spirit. How it came to realize this? Firstly, it is according to the plan of God. In her humility and in her absolute obedience she responded with the total yes "fiat". "Behold the handmaid of the Lord be it done to me according to your word.

And the "Word" became flesh and made HIS dwelling among us." Theologians called this as the mystery of the Incarnation. Isaiah the prophet fulfilled his prophecy in Jesus Christ. "The woman will conceive a child and HE is to be called the Immanuel which means "God is with us." *Our Lord continue to call all of us the Baptized. For those who grown in their personal relationship with the Lord, some are called to a noble calling to serve the Lord and His Bride, the Church.*

Let us not be tired of promoting vocations to the married life, as single blessedness, priesthood, diaconate, religious and those who will embracing the consecrated life in our Archdiocese of Edmonton. This year is being dedicated to the year of consecrated life. Let us constantly pray for our seminarians for their holy perseverance. If you felt and prayed about that you are called to the priesthood, permanent diaconate and religious life, please come to see me or our Vocation director.

Secondly, the Blessed Virgin Mary finds time for God and place God at the center of her life. God is number one in her words and actions, in everything she does. It is always for the greater glory to God. In Luke 1:35ff, our Lady's canticle of praise the "Magnificat" sums up this beautiful disposition of Mary as she said: My soul proclaims the greatness of the Lord and my spirit rejoices in God my Saviour."

Thirdly, Mary is a woman of contemplative prayer. She meditated the word of God, treasured and pondered them in her heart. In the midst of the apostles in the Upper Room, they are totally immersed in prayer which the Holy Spirit descent upon them likened to the figure of tongues of fire. Their hearts burning for the love of God and then increasingly more on fire with Divine Love, the Holy Spirit.

In human language, Mary who is not only the fairest daughter of the Eternal Father and the immaculate mother of the Incarnate Son but the virgin spouse of the Holy Spirit. She became the ark of the new covenant! *Our parish has a a unique and contemplative ambiance in meeting the Lord in the Most Holy Sacrament of the Altar exposed for an hour of Adoration and Benediction every before Mass on weekdays and on the week-ends.*

The Lord Himself appealed to his disciples at the garden of Gethsemane in these words: "Can you spend an hour with ME? The time you spent with our Eucharistic Lord, you will never regret...exchange with eternal life poured out upon us."He Himself is the oxygen of our interior life, life in the Spirit!"

Fourthly, Mary is the woman of social justice and Queen of charity. She placed into action what she believed, She walk the talk! Charity is born out of her prayers. She went with haste to the hill country side of Judea with St. Joseph riding through a donkey about 80 miles from her home Nazareth not only to visit her cousin, St. Elizabeth but to help her in her daily household chores.

Knowing that her cousin was pregnant for six months of John the Baptist. A charity without delay, she went with haste as the evangelist Luke described it. She stayed with her first cousin, Elizabeth for three months with her support and assistance.

Our Lord said: "What you have done to the least brothers and sisters of mine, you have done it to me." *In our parish today, we are lacking of volunteers under the ministry of pastoral care. Those ministering to our hospital, shut inns or nursing homes who bring Holy Communion to our elderly and sick brothers and sisters.*

Please call our parish after discerning and praying about it. God might be calling you as well to do this noble ministry. Let us imitate the Blessed Virgin Mary by doing charity to others without delay. Truly, more blessed are those who come in the name of the Lord!

In this season of advent, let us imitate the heroic virtues of the Blessed Virgin Mary our true model and guide for this beautiful season of advent. Let us implore her prayerful intercessions as she prayerfully interceded at wedding feast at Cana of Galilee.

At the unexpected hour, our Lord did perform the miracle of changing six jars of water into the most special wine, resolving the misery and disappointments of the bride and groom through our Lady's prayerful intercession.

Our life rooted in Christ truly finds more meaning and indeed becomes worth living! As we gaze upon the lowliness of Mary, she has been exalted by God and her cousin, St. Elizabeth greeted her with these words: "Blessed are you among women and blessed ifs the fruit of your womb, JESUS!"

Let us entrust our lives and loved ones to the Almighty God through the powerful intercession of Mary who is full of grace. May she dispense necessary graces not only for our holy perseverance in our journey of faith this advent and Christmas but to assist us how we can come to know deeper our Lord God.

How we can enthrone Christ as our King into our hearts, homes and entire parish community. We knew that the closest to the Sacred Heart of our Lord is no other than the Blessed Virgin Mary, let us place our confidence on her maternal love and care for us.

What a profound devotion to her, what a spiritual journey knowing that we have such a lovely mother whom Jesus entrusted at the foot of the Cross to St. John the beloved Apostle saying: "Son, behold your mother!" and in turn, he said to his own mother, "Woman behold your son!"

Like Mary, let us conceive Jesus in our mind, in our hearts and in our way of life, and living the fullness of Christian life. Truly, a life rooted in Jesus Christ is the sweetest paradise, with our Lady's assistance we are sure and certain of this reality. For through her, Christ came into our world and through her we can approach Christ the way our Blessed Mother Mary pleases him.

May your advent be a grace-filled one like that first advent when Mary declared as a woman full of grace. Amen

On Advent To Whom Are You Waiting for ? *: Is Jesus At The Center of Your Preoccupation?*

Advent is fast approaching and after four weeks of Advent, then Christmas comes. We can imagine how our world is too busy that we felt time flies and for some they are unaware that time is short and for some who are idling, time is too long.

We thank for the gift of time but above all to the author of time who Himself from eternity entered not only space and time but cloth Himself with our human nature, he took flesh in the womb of the Blessed Virgin Mary and became human like us in all things except sin. That author of time became one of us, the one who shapes our history and destiny, he walks with us, the Emmanuel who is "God with us", Jesus the Christ.

As we spend our time in prayer, fellowship with co-parishioners, hang out with friends and enjoy the company of our parents, our beloved elders, siblings and relatives, sometimes we are unaware that in the midst of us is Christ who Himself is the silent listener to every conversation, a friend companion in our journey as he said: "where two or three gathered in my name, I am in the midst of them."

The season of advent is a season of joyful anticipation of the second coming of Christ and so we need to be prayerful and vigilant. It is the season of grace and patient anticipation His birth and allowing Him to be truly born in our hearts as Christians.

Let us be grateful to God for the time we spend for our spiritual exercises, studies, apostolate, our work and above all of embracing our Catholic faith and at the heart of all these is Christ Jesus, our Lord! Let us value our faith in Him and live the virtues He taught us. I will share to you a story that could lead us to our advent reflection in the midst of the hustle -bustle of life.

A few years ago a group of salesmen went to a regional sales convention in Chicago . They had assured their wives that they would be home in plenty of time for Friday night's dinner. In their rush, with tickets and briefcases, one of
these salesmen inadvertently kicked over a table which held a display of apples. Apples flew everywhere. Without stopping or looking back, they all managed to reach the plane in time for their nearly-missed boarding...

All But One!!! He paused, took a deep breath, got in touch with his feelings and experienced a twinge of compassion for the girl whose apple stand had been overturned.

He told his buddies to go on without him, waved good-bye, told one of them to call his wife when they arrived at their
home destination and explain his taking a later flight. Then he returned to the terminal where the apples were all over
the terminal floor.

He was glad he did. The 16-year-old girl was totally blind! She was softly crying, tears running down her cheeks in

frustration, and at the same time helplessly groping for her spilled produce as the crowd swirled about her; no one
stopping and no one to care for her plight.

The salesman knelt on the floor with her, gathered up the apples, put them back on the table and helped organize her
display. As he did this, he noticed that many of them had become battered and bruised; these he set aside in another basket.

When he had finished, he pulled out his wallet and said to the girl, "Here, please take this $40 for the damage we did.
Are you okay? She nodded through her tears. He continued on with, "I hope we didn't spoil your day too badly."

As the salesman started to walk away, the bewildered blind girl called out to him, "Mister...." He paused and turned to look back into those blind eyes. She continued, "Are you Jesus?"

He stopped in mid-stride and he wondered. He gently went back and said, "No, I am nothing like Jesus - He is good, kind, caring, loving, and would never have bumped into your display in the first place.

"The girl gently nodded: "I only asked because I prayed for Jesus to help me gather the apples. He sent you to help me, so you are like Him - only He knows who will do His will. Thank you for hearing His call, Mister."

Then slowly he made his way to catch the later flight with that question burning and bouncing about in his soul: "Are you Jesus?"

Do people mistake you for Jesus?

That's our destiny, is it not? To be so much like Jesus that people cannot tell the difference as we live and interact with a world that is blind to His love, life and grace.

If we claim to know Him, we should live, walk and act as He would. Knowing Him is more than simply quoting scripture and going to Church. It's actually living the Word as life unfolds day to day.

You are the apple of His eye even though you, too, have been bruised by a fall. He stopped what He was doing and picked up you and me on a hill called Calvary and paid in full for our damaged fruit.

And so this advent especially on December 10 at 7pm, we have the great spiritual opportunity to prepare ourselves to welcome our Lord into our hearts by reconciling ourselves to God, to the Church and to one another through the sacrament of Penance or Confession. Five priests are coming to celebrate this feast of God's forgiveness and merciful love.

Give yourself a gift, a precious gift of inner peace, peace of mind and conscience, a re-awakening and cleansing of the soul whom God delights. May the Sacred vessel of the Holy Spirit which is our interior life becomes a fitting dwelling place of the Holy Spirit.

May the eternal Word of the Father may took flesh in our hearts too. Let us imitate our Blessed Mother Mary in meditating the Word in our mind, in pondering and treasuring it in our hearts, so that as we prepare our inner beings through Confession, we may become the people chosen as truly His own and find His dwelling among us. And embrace our Emmanuel: "God is with-us" Jesus Christ.

On this month of December which we are celebrating the feasts of the Immaculate Conception of the Blessed Mother Mary which is on Dec. 8 and also her title of our Lady of Guadalupe on December 12, let us ask the prayerful intercession of our Lady of Guadalupe, the Immaculate Mother of our Lord to lead us closer to the Sacred Heart of her Son, our Lord Jesus Christ.

I humbly pray that your advent be a grace-filled one and be ready to celebrate the birth of Christ in our parish, in your family above all in your soul, may Christ be truly born in your hearts. May Christ be at the heart of your Christmas celebrations which truly finds its meaning and true ambiance.

God bless you richly this joyful season of the anticipation of the coming of Christ our Lord.

Jesus Wept: *"God's Compassion Goes Beyond Our Grief & Conquered Our Death, Let Us Not Therefore Forget Our Beloved Departed"*

May the grace of consolation, sure hope and peace of the Lord be with those who are grieving at this time! November is the month of remembrance and we cannot avoid to recall how our loved ones passed away and left us suddenly or unexpectedly.

Though we are shattered by death which is un-evitable reality in our earthly sojourn, the Good Shepherd, Jesus Christ is our friend companion ushering us to the mansions of the elect in the dwellings of His eternal Father in Heaven. The Psalm 23 reminds us: "Even though I walk in the valley of darkness, I fear no evil for He is at my side." What a personal conviction and solid trust or faith in Jesus Christ!

Though Christ is Divine he is in solidarity with us, he took our human condition, clothed Himself with our human nature except sin. He understood how to be human, he allowed His Sacred Heart to be pierced by spear, he cried on the Cross for the forgiveness of our sins.

He cried thirsting for our love and our faith in Him. He wept during the death of His friend Lazarus, He wept for the Ancient Jerusalem for the people who were lack of faith in Him.

The shortest verse in the Bible is found in the Gospel of John: ***"Jesus wept."*** In the Beatitudes, our Lord invites us to enter into a beatific life and accept who we are, that we are people with emotion for natural to us to burst into tears. "Blessed are those who mourn for they shall be comforted."

Randall Roberts wrote "Shattered by Death and Strengthened by Hope employs biblical passages that can help us understand the Christian meaning of grief and how we are assured of the certain hope offered by Christ through His Cross and glorious resurrection.

According to him Grief and belief are not mutually exclusive. Grief is an appropriate response to death, even for the believer. There is "a time to weep, and a time to laugh; a time to mourn, and a time to dance" (Ecc 3:4, NRSV).

While the Christian gospel gives us great hope in the face of loss, *it does not rescue us from the pain of loss.* "Crying does not brand a griever as being weak and without faith," writes William Miller. "Experiencing and expressing feelings of anger in grief may be very appropriate and does not necessarily make one a "bad" person " (p 33).

The fact that God's people mourned at the time of death can be noted in a variety of biblical passages and stories. Consider, for example, the actions of Abraham at the time of the death of Sarah, his wife.

He "went to mourn for Sarah and to weep over her" (Gen 23:2, NIV), notes the biblical writer. Or ponder the actions of Joseph when his father Jacob died: "Joseph threw himself upon his father and wept over him and kissed him" (Gen 50:1, NIV). And what of the actions of the entire people of Israel at the death of Moses, their leader?

The Israelites grieved for Moses in the plains of Moab thirty days, until the time of weeping and mourning was over" (Dt 34:8, NIV). And our Lord himself, standing at the graveside of his friend Lazarus, and *in the full knowledge of the resurrection set to occur*, wept (See Jn 11:35).

Writing to the believers at Thessalonica, Paul urges them to consider the promise of the Lord's return and the resurrection which will then take place: "But we do not want you to be uniformed, brothers and sisters, about those who have died, *so that you may not grieve as others do who have no hope"* (1 Thess 4:13, NRSV, italics supplied).

Notice then, Paul does not use the hope of the coming of the Lord as a reason to avoid grief. Rather, he points out that a believer need not grieve *as though there is no hope.* In other words, Christian grief has a definite end. Its end is in the hope of the appearing of Christ.

It seems clear from this brief perusal of selected passages that people in Scripture sorrowed, mourned, and grieved at times of loss. Should less be expected of contemporary believers in their times of bereavement?

Might grieving Christians experience despair? The very meaning of the word despair implies that one has lost all hope. The weekend of Christ's crucifixion and death was one of inexpressible agony and pain for His disciples. Their despair was great. "With the death of Christ the hopes of His disciples perished" (White, 1940,p 772).

Such feelings of despair were aptly described by two disciples on their way to Emmaus at the end of that weekend: "But we had hoped that he was the one to redeem Israel" (Lk 24:21, NRSV, italics supplied).

The past tense of the verse implies that their hope was a thing of the past, leaving them in despair. Their words likely describe the feelings of all of Christ's followers at the time. "All our hopes were focused on Him, now that he has died, we are in despair."

Peter, who had greater reason to feel despair than any other follower of Christ, later wrote: "Blessed be the God and Father of our Lord Jesus Christ! By his great mercy he has given us a new birth into a living hope through the resurrection of Jesus Christ from the death" (1 Pet 1:3, NRSV).

Clearly, the end of his grief was founded upon the reality of Christ's resurrection and the wonderful hope it provides for believers. However, it required the mercy of God to move him from despair to hope. The reality of Christ's resurrection made hope possible against the backdrop of profound disillusionment and despair.

Those who have experienced despair--*the absence of confidence in the future*--at its most bitter can often be those for whom hope--*faith in the future*--can be the most sweet. In fact, hope *need not* be a denial of despair; rather, it can be the *answer* to despair.

It thus becomes possible to support grieving persons through the profundity of pain with a view toward ultimately securing them in hope. This takes the Christian beyond the psychological perspective of death as simply "another stage of life" which much be accepted, to recognizing death as "the last enemy" which will ultimately be destroyed (cf 1 Cor 15:26).

It is in Christ's ultimate overthrow of this enemy that we can find hope, and it is in the One who has conquered their enemy that our faith in the future--*our hope*--rests.

May our Lord Jesus Christ transform your grief and sufferings into a blessing, your defeat into victory, death into the glory of resurrection and finally open the gates of paradise where he ascended into the heavens seated at the right hand of the eternal Father.

May your grieving find its meaning in our faith in Jesus Christ who assured us: "Do not let your hearts be troubled, trust in God still and also trust in Me." Amen

As a parish community filled with faith and God's steadfast love, I cordially invite all of you to come and celebrate the feast of Christ the King on November 22, which on that day we offer the Holy Mass for the eternal repose of all our faithful departed and also for family members to be comforted by the love of our God who is rich in mercy and full of gentleness.

I humbly implore God's manifold blessings to all of you that come from the Sacred Heart of our Lord!

*"**Lest We Forget:** Christ Is the Source of True Freedom"*

November is a month of remembrance. A grace-filled month wherein we recall in a prayerful manner those who have gone before us, not only our loved ones but those who worked hard for our freedom, peace and liberty. Above all we do not forget what God has done for us, as our national Anthem says: "God keep our land, glorious and free!"

Our Lord Jesus at his last supper concluded with this important note: "Do this in remembrance of Me." Our heroes and heroines who fought for our independence, democracy and freedom that bore fruit to justice and peace in our land today has a significant impact in our lives today not only individually but as a nation. Whether it is socially, politically, financially or economically and also spiritually.

In religious context, Christ's Last supper and his Cross and resurrection has led us to a greater meaning of a sense of freedom. Freedom from Satan, father of lies and darkness, freedom from all enslavement and oppression of evil, sickness, sin and the last enemy that our Victor-King has conquered was death through his glorious resurrection. Indeed Christ our Lord has paid our salvation with the price of his life, his blood was shed on the Cross, and his Sacred Heart was wounded, pierced by a lance or spear.

This spiritual freedom was granted by the Eternal Father who never spared His Only Begotten Son to die on the Cross for you and me to have that freedom as indeed adopted sons and daughters of the Lord. ***"For God so loved the world that He gave us His Only Begotten Son, that whoever believes in Him may not die or perish but have an everlasting life."*** John 3:16.

This month of November, we honour as well our peace keeping forces, our soldiers, those in the military service, such as in the RCMP, police force, navy, air force and even our veterans who tirelessly fought for our freedom, justice and peace which we are enjoying today. Let us pray also for the eternal repose for those who have died in war for their eternal repose. The Church liturgical calendar has a special place for them. November 1 is the feast of all the Saints and the 2nd is the feasts of all the Souls.

This month, we recall the three spheres of the Church, namely: We, who are struggling against the forces of evil in the world, vigilant with our prayers and clothing ourselves with faith, the robe of salvation through baptism, we are called the "Militant Church."

Those who are under purification and undergoing the process of perfection to go to heaven with sure hope are called souls in purgatory, the "Suffering Church" and finally as arriving to our ultimate destiny and homeland, heaven, we call: the "Church Triumphant" through the merits of the passion, death and resurrection of Christ.

In the epistles St. Paul repeatedly speaks about "putting on Christ", clothing ourselves in him. It all has to do with clothing our heart and soul with Christ's attitudes toward others, with His ways of treating others... clothing ourselves with His respect for them, because they are God's children too.

In the rite of baptism we hear the priest say: "Receive this white garment, the outward sign of your Christian dignity..." Note that this outward sign is to be a window through which others see our inner selves. Through it they can see what's in our hearts and what's in our soul, see what's really in us and who we are.

One time a person asked me, what is the significance of the white cloth placed upon the casket of the deceased? I told him that it is equivalent to the white garment when you received the Sacrament of Baptism. It is the robe of salvation.

I had an experience entering the synagogues, majid, mosques, churches, shrines and basilicas when I took the course on Christianity and world religions and deepened my understanding when I did the pilgrimages in the Holy Land and Europe.

At the entrance door they display the dress code both what is proper and what is not before entering the sacred place of worship. In fact, you need to wash yourself first. Our external disposition speaks also of our internal disposition, our interior life, but we are not here to judge the book by its cover, we are promoting reverence and cultivating the ambiance of respect and prayerful disposition and love for God.

The book of revelation describes the multitudes wearing white robes and with palm branches in their hands, this speaks about the martyrs, the saints who are victorious and also our future destiny in heaven. But let us begin our journey of heaven here on earth by remembering the good deeds of those who live their lives to the fullest in Jesus Christ.

As we honour and remember them with due reverence, let us imitate their courage to live the faith and the Christian virtues they lived by, even to the point of shedding their blood.

Let us learn from their wisdom and live their heroism and legacy left for us to perpetuate and to safeguard. May their light continue to shine to us, so that we may too become the model and guide for the next generation and be the beacon of hope for others to follow.

Finally, we can make a difference in making our world today a better place to live in. Let us not forget them, let us salute them, let us honour them with pride. Indeed, blessed are the peace makers for they are to be called "children of God "! To God be the glory! Amen

"**Give Back To God**: *Gratitude Is the Language of Our Mission*"

On behalf of the Parish Community of Sacred Heart, Wetaskiwin, I would like to thank you most sincerely for all your hard work and dedication in promoting the three major pastoral priorities of our Archdiocese as the priorities of our parish too (Faith formation, New Evangelization and Fostering the Culture of Vocations), but above all, the services you have done for our parish.

Thank you for all your extra work and apostolate that you are so humble that some of your work are done unnoticed. Thanks for your humility and zeal for souls. You become the source of inspirations for others.

Besides you have the courage in responding to the call of God in whatever ministry you are called for in our parish as we are promoting the spirituality of stewardship. Your time devoted, the talents and treasures which you had wholeheartedly shared.

To name some few... cleaning the Church and sacristy, the ground and the Church yard, washing the dishes, making Prayer Shawls, being sacristans, helping our youth ministry, being Lectors, Extra-Ordinary Ministers of Communion, Pastoral Care, operating the Overhead projector, visiting the sick at the hospitals, responding to the call of social justice, and other Liturgical Ministries, etc... is highly appreciated.

As advocates in promoting the Time, Talent and Treasures in our parish ministry is indeed a great manifestation of living out the life of good stewardship. On this month of October of our thanksgiving, allow me to express my sincere gratitude.

Thank you very much dear parishioners for your generosity and cheerfulness in serving God through Sacred Heart Parish. Thank you for being there at our appreciation night last October 9. May the Almighty God enrich you with the abundance of His grace and blessings!

This week is the World Mission Sunday and all of us the baptized are consecrated for the mission of the Church. God has called us in a unique way, and whenever we are working, we are called to be the salt of the earth and light to the nations.

Charity begins at home and here in our parish. To continue this mission, I humbly appeal to you to please donate not only your time and talent but if possible financially which we are in dire need of money.

The envelop on the pews awaits a cheerful and generous benefactors like you. We are almost done with our Cathedraticum of $57,000 dollars. Besides, we have new roof for our rectory, brand new chairs and well furnished parish hall and a lot of faith formation programs in various ages especially our youth ministry program.

The Church by nature is missionary and without your help and financial support how can we continue and move forward? I would like you to reflect on the poem written by **St.Teresa of Avila (1515–1582),** Carmelite nun, mystic and great doctor of the Church:

"Christ Has No Body "

Christ has no body but yours,
No hands, no feet on earth but yours,
Yours are the eyes with which he looks
Compassion on this world,
Yours are the feet with which he walks to do good,
Yours are the hands, with which he blesses all the world.
Yours are the hands, yours are the feet,
Yours are the eyes, you are his body.
Christ has no body now but yours,
No hands, no feet on earth but yours,
Yours are the eyes with which he looks
compassion on this world.
Christ has no body now on earth but yours.

May God bless all of you in every good deeds that you render to the Church in the name of Christ. I humbly invoke the unfailing help and strength the comes from the Holy Spirit.

You may be refreshed by the presence of the Holy Spirit, the sweetest guest of every soul as we embark for another Life in the Spirit Retreat this week. Thank you! Thank you! Thank you all!

"**Honour Your Mother**: *Mary, the Mother of Christ, Mother of the Church*"

September 8 is the feast of the nativity of the Blessed Virgin Mary, mother of our Lord and Saviour, Jesus Christ. How do we know that? Tradition of the Church declares that the Immaculate Conception of our Blessed Virgin Mary happened in the womb of her mother, St. Anne on December 8.

Thus, we count 9 months forward and appropriated approximately September 8 is the solemnity of the Blessed Virgin Mary's birthday. There are only three birthdays celebrated within the liturgical calendar of the Church, firstly, our Lord's on Dec. 25, then our Lady's which is this forth coming September 8 and thirdly, St. John the Baptist on June 24 and nothing more.

On this month of her birthday, how do we honour her? Do we heed her call and her request about the first Saturday devotion to her Immaculate Heart during her apparition in the Cova di Iria, Fatima, Portugal in 1917? And how important it is?

The Consecration of the entire universe including Russia to her Immaculate Heart shapes the history of the world. Berlin Wall has been destroyed to unite Germany from East to West, John Paul II was spared from the assassination attempts, Mikael Gorbachev met John Paul II prior to meet US President Ronald Reagan.

Communism in Europe opened the door to peace and freedom. The two children visionaries, Francisco and his sister Jacinta were beatified by Pope John Paul II and Lucia their first cousin entered religious life and now awaits the process to be beatified as well. The triumph of the Immaculate Heart has been revealed and so Marian Year had been declared by the Popes of our century and celebrated with fervent devotion.

The Sacred Scriptures or the Holy Bible calls her the New Eve, mother of many nations and indeed she is blessed among women, full of grace. The Torah of the Jewish People had recognized Mary as the daughter of Zion, the Koran of the Islam mentioned her several times and she is known as "Mariam" which means "Star of the Sea."

As we venerate Mary, the mother of our Lord, she is also our mother because at the foot of the Cross, she stood there and Jesus declared to St. John the beloved Apostle who represents not only the apostles but the Church, saying: "Son, behold your mother!"

As Jesus inaugurated the new family and the reign Kingdom of God, the ever-Virgin Mary has a special place in the Sacred Heart of God. God Himself commands: "Honour your father and your mother." Above all earthly parents and authorities, the Blessed Virgin Mary has the special place not only in our Church but worthy of our veneration and honour as disciples of Christ.

It is unthinkable for a follower of Christ to be a faithful disciple of our Lord without respect and due honour to Mary, the mother of our Saviour, Jesus Christ!

The most ancient motto of our Church: "AD JESUM PER MARIAM" which means "All to Jesus through Mary." The papacy of St. John Paul II was aided by the powerful intercession of our Lady as his motto states: "Totus Tous, Maria" which means "I am totally yours, Oh Mary!" Truly he is the saint of the Blessed Mother Mary.

As faithful disciples of Christ, let us learn from the wisdom of our Lady, she placed Jesus at the center of her life, she pondered everything in her Immaculate Heart even those things that she cannot totally understand in the course of her life. It was the Heart of Mary which expressed her "yes" to God.

This was her response to the message sent through the angel at the Annunciation. By her loving consent, Mary first conceived Christ in her heart and then in her womb. Our Lord Jesus, Himself: when reminded by a woman in the crowd how blessed was the womb which gave birth to Him, responds, "Blessed rather are those who hear the word of God and keep it." (Lk. 11:28)

Pope John Paul II, in his first encyclical, *Redemptor Hominis*, wrote "the mystery of Redemption was formed under the heart of the Virgin of Nazareth when she pronounced her 'fiat.'" (R.H. #22) "Behold the handmaid of the Lord, be it done to me according to your word, says, Mary.

Devotion to Mary's Immaculate Heart has a greater flowering following the manifestation of the Miraculous Medal to St. Catherine Laboure in 1830 and the Appearances of' Our Lady in Fatima. From May 13 to October 13, 1917, our Blessed Mother Mary appeared to three children, Jacinta and Francisco Marto and their cousin Lucia Dos Santos in Fatima, Portugal. On July 13 she told them: "to save poor sinners, God wishes to establish in the world devotion to my Immaculate Heart." The entire Fatima message is one of prayer, penance and making sacrifices and reparation to God for the many offenses against Him.

In 1942, the twenty-fifth anniversary of Fatima, Pope Pius XII consecrated the world to the Immaculate Heart of Mary. That same year, he assigned the feast day to August 22, the octave of the Assumption.

On May 4, 1944, he extended the Feast of the Immaculate Heart of Mary to the Universal Church. With the liturgical reforms of the Second Vatican Council in 1969, the feast was given a more suitable place on the day following the Feast of the Sacred Heart of Jesus. That is the Saturday after the second Sunday after Pentecost.

As devotees of the Sacred Heart of Jesus, let us open our hearts to the devotion to the Immaculate Heart of Mary who can lead us to the center of all hearts, the most Loving Heart of God.

Beginning First Saturday (6th) of September 2014 at 9a.m., let us celebrate our Lady's Saturday, a Holy Mass in honour of the Immaculate Heart of Mary in the Parish of the Most Sacred Heart Church, Wetaskiwin, Alberta.

Let us consecrate ourselves, members of our respective family, the entire parish, the surrounding missions and the entire universe to the Immaculate Heart of Mary, mother of our Lord.

This is a historical event, please come let us sing together the Magnificat of Mary, her song of praise: "My soul proclaims the greatness of the Lord, my spirit rejoices in God my Saviour!' Immaculate Heart of Mary, pray for us! Amen

"**Faith Matters**: *Without Faith, We Can Not Please God, Seek God First*"

St. James reminds us that faith without good works is dead and above all without faith we cannot please God. One of the major pastoral priorities of our parish and of our archdiocese is faith formation.

I would say, education in faith is from womb to tomb, indeed it is a lifetime process. If our Lord Jesus went home to Nazareth after he was found in the temple when he was twelve and he was described in the gospel that he was raised by Blessed Mary and St. Joseph that he grew in knowledge, in size, in wisdom and in God's grace and so, are we?

Faith formation is indeed essential in our prayer life and growth in the spirit, hoping that our Mother Church continue to teach and nourish us with the substance of truth and sanctifying grace necessary for our salvation. The trees, grass, plants and vegetation in the fields and mountains continue to grow because of the dew, the rain , the moist and the sun and the nutrients of the field.

Thought the farmers are unaware that the seeds sprout and time flies the fruits and vegetables are ready to be harvested. Grace builds in nature and yet we have a supernatural life as Christ encourages us to walk in faith and grow together as members of His Mystical Body on earth, the Church.

Seek first the Kingdom of God, Jesus said and everything shall be added unto you, I will add to that, and on the top of it is life of abundance, eternal happiness. The time you spent with Christ in prayer and faith formation are not wasted, in fact Christ will exchange it with eternity, eternal life! Growing in faith is the joy of the soul and delightful to the Lord. Who among parents are not happy seeing their children growing, achieving their goal in life, finishing their studies? And so, above all with God, our Eternal Father.

Investing in spiritual riches and personal growth and friendship with God, no money can buy, no inflation can obstruct. And so, for your well being and wholesome experience of joy which is coming from God, I highly encourage you to sign up and you will not regret at the end. Like that of St. Paul, he said: " I have kept the faith, I have fought the good fight, I have ran the race, now. I am about to reach the finish line, I knew that there's a crown that awaits for me, a crown that never withers, a crown of victory, a crown of eternal life."

As we seek the Kingdom of God here on earth as our first priority as we love God above all, our labors will not be in vain, in fact, it is rewarding. St. Augustine once said: "My heart is restless until I find rest, content and happiness in you alone my God!"

May the goodness, beauty and richness of our Catholic and Apostolic faith handed by our Lord to us through the apostles make you docile and vibrant members of his Kingdom which we need to belong and may you find the true wealth and eternal happiness that nobody can snatch away.

"Peace is my gift says the Lord, my peace I give to you which the world can never give." May the peace of mind and conscience be with you as you make efforts in deepening your friendship with God through these faith formation in our parish here at Sacred Heart, Wetaskiwin.

To embark in building up God's Kingdom, planting the indestructible seed of our faith to our young people, who comprise the Church of today and tomorrow is crucial in our journey of faith in our parish today. I need your collaboration and all out support.

We have the new youth minister, Christina Fernandez who is so talented, truly a gift from the Lord. Despite of many challenges not only in the lives of our young people but of every family. God can make a way to bridge the home, the school and the parish and one of the hope that God has given us is the energetic youth minister who will be ministering to our young people in school and in our parish.

I encourage our school staff and teachers, parents and guardians and all our parishioners to collaborate and work together for the spiritual growth of our children. The future of our land and of the Church depends on our young people, the future leaders, the fair hope of the Kingdom of God.

In our life time, let us ask ourselves what we have done, what we have contributed in building up God's Kingdom today and tomorrow? God will make all things beautiful, enriched and orderly in His time. And so, our Lord taught us that time is a gift and precious. As we do God's will here on earth we also accomplish things in heaven as well, and so we do not waste our time.

We are called to be good stewards. Can you share your time, talent and treasures in building up the Kingdom of God through our parish youth ministry? At the end of our earthly pilgrimage, we are sure that we have the answer that can satisfy the Lord and pleasing to Him. The answer is in your heart.

May the Lord embrace you with the sweetness of His love, provide all your needs according to His riches and glory through Christ, our Lord. Amen God bless you all!

"If You Love Me Then You Will Follow My Commands: *Some Friendly Reminders At Liturgical Celebrations Out Of Love For Jesus"*

The great poet says: "A thing of beauty is a joy forever." The psalmist declares: "In God's time, He makes all things beautiful," and so we need to be patient. Indeed, we cannot thank God more than enough for the wonder and beauty of His creation and the beauty and sweetness of His love and care for us! Pope Emeritus, Benedict XVI said: "There's nothing more beautiful than to be surprised by the Gospel and to tell others about our friendship with Jesus Christ. We are then called to evangelize and bring others to Jesus.

I was reminded by one of the momentous spiritual journey of mine in the Holy Land during the year of priests in June 2010. As we come to venerate the sacred place of "Caenaculum" the Upper Room where the Last Supper happened and the outpouring of the Holy Spirit during the Pentecost, I noticed that on the post or the arches by the door was the engraved " Pelican" mother bird that feeds her brood with her own very substance of blood from her breast.

What an image that speaks of love and care of a mother who sacrifice so much of herself for the sake of life, nourishment, nurturance, growth and love for kids and family. This image speaks of God's love for us poured out in the Sacraments especially in the Mass, the Holy Eucharist, where Christ over flowingly generous, saying: "This is my Body...my Blood poured out for you...."

Through Christ, God has nourished us with His very substance, Body, Blood, Soul and Divinity. In the mystery of Communion which is the essence of the Church, Christ declares: "The Father is in Me and I in the Father, I and the Father are One." And so the mystery of the sacrament especially the Eucharist speaks also so profound that when we receive the Lord through Holy Communion. He has given us not only food for our spiritual journey but His Divine substance that one day we may have glorified bodies like His, truly Risen from the dead.

Christ is not only within us and among us but we are in Him, we are in the Holy Trinity who made His dwelling firstly in our Baptism, immersed totally in His Divine Life and the sanctifying grace poured out upon us. We need to value the Sacraments instituted not by human hands but by God Himself in Jesus Christ. We need to embrace the Church and her teachings since She is the Bride of Christ, and through her we are reborn in the spirit and becoming new creation in Christ.

Christ relationship with his Bride, the Church is indissoluble and inseparable which St. Paul reminded married couples to do the same. It is only through God's love and grace that the bond of marriage is being strengthened more. How do we encounter the Lord in an excellent way if we don't go to Church? Direct from the lips of Christ, "Upon this Rock, I will build my Church." (Mt. 16:13-20). ***"Where two or three gathered in my name, I am in the midst of them and I will be with you always until the end of the world."*** (Mt. 28:19).

As we gather together every Sunday in the Mass, do we really believe that Christ is in our midst? I am the Living Bread that has come down from heaven, "take and eat, this is my Body, take and drink, this is my blood"...do we really believe that the one who invites us is Jesus and not only that, what He is giving us is His very substance?

Do we really believe and embrace the magisterial teaching of the Church on the real presence of Christ especially in the Eucharist? Do we really say "Amen!" when we receive Jesus through holy communion? Do we express our reverence by bowing before the presence of Eucharistic Lord? Do we genuflect before the Blessed Sacrament or when Christ is exposed in the Blessed Sacrament of the Holy Altar? Do we knell during the consecration as an utmost expression of or reverence and belief in the true presence of the Lord?

By our gestures, it deeply manifests our interior disposition so much so that it is cultivated by our interior prayerful silence. "Of course we cannot judge the book by its cover!" We strive to catechize our lapse Catholic brothers and sisters with gentleness and compassion especially at funerals who are chewing gum and receiving the Bread of Life, Jesus in Holy Communion. It is a form of desecration and it is an abomination to chew gum with the sacred Body and precious Blood of Christ at the same time!

All the baptized are responsible to educate and to instruct the ignorant as one of the spiritual works of mercy. We also encourage our beloved to have at least modest vests in approaching the Lord. Another thing is a Eucharistic fast at least an hour prior to Holy Communion that means no food before Mass unless someone is under medical condition.

This instruction is not for the sake of restrictions or legalities but out of love for our Lord Jesus Christ who comes to us through the Sacraments and for someone to prosper in his or her spiritual well being. For Christ Himself said: "If you love Me, then you will follow my commands."

Reception of holy communion should be consumed in front of the minister. If it is received by hands, and if you are right handed, let the left hand be on top of your right since your right hand will pick up for communion. The sacred left over on your palm should be consumed as well if there are crumbs, we do it very reverently. We need to safeguard the Holy Eucharist, not only by the priest, deacon or extra-ordinary ministers of Holy Communion but by every baptized person.

For those who are non-Catholic and Catholic faithful who examined their conscience that knowing that they are not in the state of grace to receive Holy Communion, we appreciate their spiritual honesty and so I advise them to pray the Act of Spiritual Communion Prayer. And finally, advising them if they can approach the sacrament of penance/ confession 30 minutes prior to the Mass.

Act of Spiritual Communion
by St. Alphonsus Ligouri

My Jesus,
I believe that You
are present in the Most Holy Sacrament.
I love You above all things,
and I desire to receive You into my soul.
Since I cannot at this moment
receive You Sacramentally,
come at least spiritually into my heart. I embrace You as if You were already there and unite myself wholly to You. Never permit me to be separated from You.
Amen.

Your cooperation is sincerely appreciated. Parents of children who are communicants should be with them to assist them to be sure that what they learned from sacramental preparation is being executed and applied in the reception of Holy Communion. If they forgot to say, Amen, they should kindly teach them as well.

We need to put off our cell phones, tablets and other gadgets and put off our outdoor hats as well when Mass is going on. We need to listen to the one voice, the voice of the Lord. Distraction is one of the enemies of prayer and contemplative life. We support each other in our spiritual growth and to have an interior life rooted in our communion with Christ and his Church.

When we are giving the sign of peace, we are advised not to go around. We shake hands to those who are close and accessible to us and refrain from loud noise which can disrupt the solemnity of the Holy Mass. You may have fellowship after Mass if you wish to congregate again in our parish hall to have time for one another. That's another dimension of our communion to one another, its social aspect for a deeper fellowship.

Above all, we encourage you to spend a silent adoration of the Blessed Sacrament after Mass to sink in the grace and to ponder the great mystery we have just received and celebrated. We need to respect others who are praying inside the Church. The Foyer is also a venue for us to greet people and also to enjoy the pan cake breakfast with our brother Knights of Columbus at the hall.

I don't mind children are crying in our Church, they are the hope of the Church of today and tomorrow, but if the child is crying out loud that can disrupt the Mass, we encourage parents and ushers to let them be brought at the crying room or foyer for the time being and if they are in quiet moment they may return to their designated pews or wherever they are seated. All children are always welcome to the children's liturgy and now to our Vacation Bible School.

Our Lord Jesus is always saying: "Let the little children come to me, unless you become little children, you will never enter the Kingdom of God." We encourage parents sometimes to be with their kids during the children's liturgy so that they have some ideas what's going on or they can make some suggestions for the spiritual growth of our young children.

I also invite you to sign up for adoration for our parish youth, we need your moral, financial and prayerful support. We ask the Lord through the intercession of St. Philomena for the future of our youth ministry to blossom and prosper in our church and in our school. Your collaboration for the future of our Church, where God is leading us is gratefully appreciated.

Thanks for your patience, love, care and understanding in building up the Kingdom of God. What we had sown, we will reap. If we sow the seed of faith and immortality then we will reap eternal life and everlasting happiness in heaven. Please help us plant the seed of faith so that at the spring time of our spiritual life, you may reap the copious harvest of eternal life in Jesus Christ, our Lord. Amen.

With my fervent prayers and priestly counsel, I humbly remain in the Most Sacred Heart of Jesus.

"Let Summer Intensify Our Friendship with God Whose Creation Undeniably Speaks the Beauty of His Love: *God's Grace Is Truly Built On Nature"*

Summer has arrived and we welcome our guests and visitors attending to the Lord's through silent adoration and Masses here at Sacred Heart Parish. As a parish community striving to be a witness to live the life of Christ in abundance, we need to pause a moment of prayerful silence this summer by examining our lives. This is a life living the spirit of Stewardship. We value time, talents, treasures and relationships and the heart of these is God, author and lover of life.

The Greek philosopher, Socrates once said: "The unexamined life is not worth living." The beauty of nature around us serves as a wonderful ambiance to encounter the Creator, our Lord God. Even during winter times, the snow speaks of the purity of God and with prophet Daniel we pray with him through the liturgy of the hours saying: "Ice and snow bless the Lord, cold and chill bless the Lord," and so with the beautiful summer days when the sun smile upon us.

Are we not gracious and grateful?! Let us open our eyes to the wonder of God's goodness and love for us! We should be grateful in small things and big things as well, of little miracles happening in our lives, family, school and Church.

This is the season of grace and this is not the reason that we cannot attend the very source and summit of our Christian life, the Eucharist. The more we encounter God in the wonder of nature, His creation, the more we long to meet Him and nourish ourselves by the one who communicates Himself in love, Jesus Christ in the Eucharist. King David, in the psalms unceasingly longing for God as he said: "Like the deer that yearns for running streams, so my soul longs for you Oh Lord, my God."

Well, wherever you go, be mindful of the Lord first. Try to plan ahead where you can attend Mass on Sundays. Try to go to our Archdiocesan website and there you can see different parishes and Mass times posted." Seek first the Kingdom of God, our Lord Jesus said and everything shall be added unto you."

The time you spend with God in nature and intensified further in the grace of the Eucharist which we allowed ourselves to be nourished with, is indeed a wholesome thing to do and for us to advance in grace and to bloom in our spiritual life. The time you spent with God, no money can never buy, no amount can equate.

In fact, God can exchange it with eternity, eternal life! You will never regret of devoting your time with God and with the Church which Christ has founded. Indeed, we are not only called to become good stewards of time, but we are called to be stewards of a balance life.
"A sound mind in a healthy body." And we need to look after our body, physical welfare and more so with our spiritual well being, our friendship and personal relationship with God.

St. Paul said based on his journey of faith: "If God is for us who can be against us, and who can separate us from His love?". And finally, he said: "It is no longer I who lives but is Christ who lives in me."

The Holy Eucharist is the supreme act of thanksgiving to God, we need to bring others and encourage them to participate actively. Parents and guardians have a deep responsibility towards all those God has entrusted to them to bring them to the light of faith and to practice it.

For without faith, we cannot please God. This is a gesture of our Christian faith to be grateful for all the blessings and the life that God has bestowed upon us, we go to Church and participate actively and also to do the acts of charity.

In the Eucharistic celebration, we continually lifting our hearts to God, a constant practice how we can ascend to the heights of sanctity, called to be saints, heroes and heroines of our faith. Since Jesus inaugurated the kingdom of God, his new family, we dare to call God, our Father.

He taught us the Lord's Prayer direct from his lips, our hands during the Mass should be in "orans position" which means in "a praying hand" for the minister or priest who administer the Mass lifting all our prayers by lifting his hands up high to the Father, acting "in persona Christi capitis" which means in the person of Christ, the head of the Body, the Church.

And furthermore, during the consecration, we knell down in humble adoration, acknowledging the real presence of Christ which we believe happens at the consecration. As I observed during funerals and weddings, some are chewing gum and I don't know if it is for medical reasons, even that should not chew gums with the reception of Holy Communion.

In fact, we need to have a Eucharistic fast at least an hour prior to Holy Communion. This is my priestly advice as we sincerely believe in the real presence (Body, Blood, Soul and Divinity) of our Lord Jesus Christ in the Eucharist. we just celebrated the solemnity of the feast of His Body and Blood, the Corpus Christi.

It was a grace moment that in our parish, we were able to discuss all these things during the workshop with the New Roman Missal and with its GIRM, "General Instructions of Roman Missal" last year.

Thank you for all your wonderful contributions in building up the Kingdom of God and edifying the Church, Christ's Body through your time, talents and treasures shared with us. Truly, the Most Sacred Heart of the Lord will continually burning with the fire of love for you and me as we learn from each other and walk together in the WAY of Christ. Have a blessed summer and fruitful holidays in the Lord, God bless you and your family!

Rediscover The Richness of The Devotion To The Most Sacred Heart of Jesus:
"The Center of All Hearts"

The Most Sacred Heart of Jesus burning for love for us and unceasingly consecrating us to the truth will never deceive Himself nor deceive us. Christ who is the Way, the Truth, and the Life is ushering us to enter into the glory of the Eternal Father. He who Himself is the fullness of truth will fulfill His promises to us.

There are twelve promises of the Most Sacred Heart that we need to focus and meditate not only of First Fridays but an art of living them daily so that we may have life in abundance as Christ promised us. One of these moving promises of our Lord is that:

"I promise you in the excessive mercy of my Heart that my all-powerful love will grant to all those who receive Holy Communion on the First Fridays in nine consecutive months the grace of final perseverance; they shall not die in my disgrace, nor without receiving their sacraments. My divine Heart shall be their safe refuge in this last moment" (Jesus to St. Margaret Mary).

Sixteenth century Calvinism and seventeenth century Jansenism preached a distorted Christianity that substituted for God's love and sacrifice of His Son for all men the fearful idea that a whole section of humanity was inexorably damned.

The Church always countered this view with the infinite love of our Saviour who died on the Cross for all humanity on Good Friday. The institution of the feast of the Sacred Heart was soon to contribute to the creation among the faithful of a powerful current of devotion which since then has grown steadily stronger.

The first Office and Mass of the Sacred Heart were composed by St. John Eudes, but the institution of the feast was a result of the appearances of our Lord to St. Margaret Mary Alacoque in 1675.

The celebration of the feast was extended to the general calendar of the Church by Pius IX in 1856. Here in our parish in Wetaskiwin, we honor the Most Sacred Heart with fervent devotion not only on first Fridays but every hour prior to every Mass with humble adoration and benediction and a twenty four hours of exposition and adoration on the first Thursday and Friday of every month.

This is a profound expression of our pious love for our God whose heart was wounded by a lance and yet it is the great paradox that by his wounded Heart we are healed and by His death we are assured of a certain hope that in Christ we become a new creation looking forward to eternal life and happiness.

Let us rejoice and celebrate our feast day with fervent devotion to the center of all hearts, the Most Sacred Heart of Jesus. He invites us to learn from Him for He is gentle, meek and humble of heart. Happy feast day and may the loving heart of our Lord will never stop loving you and your respective families. May His grace and loving mercy abounds in our faith communities here in our parish in Wetaskiwin.

As dynamic and vibrant parish, let us always be grateful for the working of the Holy Spirit and the fire of the love of the Most Sacred Heart of Jesus. Let us continue to open the Church door of our parish, open wide to Christ in the disguise of the strangers, the poor, the faint hearted, the destitute, the grieving and the needy.

May the pastoral or episcopal visit of our Auxiliary Bishop, Most Reverend Gregory Bittman be a moment of grace for us especially in executing the three major pastoral priorities of our Archdiocese within our parish. Your collaboration for the love of God is always appreciated and gratefully acknowledged.

We are also blessed by our energetic pastoral staff and as a team working hard for the glory of our Lord and for the salvation of souls and in partner with our new set of PPC officers and members at large who work hard with utmost charity without delay. For in Christ, with Christ and through Christ nothing is impossible, to Him all honour, glory and praise now and forever. Amen

Most Sacred Heart of Jesus, gentle, meek and humble of Heart, make our hearts like Yours!

Holy Eucharist The Pledge of Eternal Life: "*Let Us Begin Our Heaven On Earth Through Worthy Reception of Holy Communion*"

Prayerful greetings to all our first communicants together with all their respective parents. Likewise, to those who were instrumental in catechizing them and be ever ready spiritually, our school teachers, mentors, grandparents and our parish staff and pastoral assistant.

Congratulations to all of you communicants for the first time, and may Christ who is absolutely present in the Sacraments nourishing you with His own Divine Word that leads us to everlasting life. Not only that, but by His precious Body, Blood, Soul and Divinity in a par excellent way in the Eucharist, in the Holy Communion.

This is the excellent way of receiving Him. This is not a lip service of accepting Him as one's personal Lord and Saviour, but a solid faith in Him who instituted the Sacraments and established His One Church is gratuitous to be with us and as a food for our spiritual journey to heaven.

In Holy Communion we are one and united with and in Christ. Christ is in you and you are in Christ, truly a Holy Communion, what a beautiful mystical experience for you dear young people! The grace that you will receive is overflowing. Christ Himself in the Eucharist is not only the very source of our Christian life but the pledge of eternal glory.

"Take and receive, this is my Body, this is my Blood poured out for you and for many for the forgiveness of sins." And it is a command, "Do this...." Christ who is the Way, the Truth and the Life offers Himself, He cannot deceive us nor deceive Himself since He is the absolute truth and whose nature and essence is TRUTH.

If our parents and grandparents know what is best for us children and grand kids, the Holy Mother Church knows much better what is best for our sanctification and eternal salvation, Christ Himself truly present in the Holy Eucharist.

Christ Himself is our manna, the "Living Bread" that has come down from heaven and furthermore, Christ Himself exhorts us: "He who eats my flesh and drinks my blood, I will raise them up on the last day."(See John 6).

It is the glorified Body of Christ whom we receive in the Eucharist, a body that never touch by decay and no corruption can ever touch. No wonder that we have litany of several saints that they themselves whose bodies were incorruptible, that scientists today marvel and cannot fully comprehend.

Is this not the efficacy of the Holy Eucharist of Christ Himself who is risen from the dead? Don't regret to offer your time with Christ in prayer especially in attending Mass every Sunday, Christ will exchange it with eternal life. Time is too short, eternity has no beginning and no end, regret comes last. Let us celebrate our faith in Christ who can transform our mortality to immortality, our trials into blessings, our defeat into victory, our death to resurrection and temporal life to eternal life!

Truly, a life rooted in Christ is a life of heaven, a life in abundance, the sweetest paradise! So, my dear young friends please attend the Mass and nourish yourselves with food that never spoil, food that last to eternal life. No food can satiate our spiritual journey except the Body and Blood of Christ in the Eucharist.

Even the entire universe be flooded by bakeshops that bake special bread, it can never equate even with just a single piece of a consecrated host, the Body of Christ. Always invite your siblings, relatives, friends and above all your parents to come to Church every Sunday, surely Jesus will smile upon you and ever be gracious to you.

Who can store up graces for your bright future, brighter than the sun of the day light? Only our Lord Jesus Christ, come to Him in prayer everyday and nourish yourselves with the Eucharist every Sunday.

May the fire of love of God be in your hearts burning intensely...for we cannot thank God more than enough and even more we do not deserve His blessings if we know how to examine humbly ourselves of who we are ? We are poor creatures, we are mere beggars before God's awesome and amazing presence who gave Himself totally not only on the Altar of the Cross but also on the Altar of the Word and of the Holy Eucharist.

"Oh Sacrament most holy, Oh Sacrament Divine, all praise and all thanksgiving be every moment Thine! And how holy is this feast, Christ is our spiritual food and nourishment on our pilgrimage to eternal life in God's kingdom in heaven. Amen!"

Again, congratulations and may God delights in you and may the "Emmanuel" find His dwelling deep within you, God loves you dearly! I humbly invoke His blessings to all of you and to your family!

Flores de Mayo: ***"My Childhood Devotion To the Most Holy Mother of God"***

Allow me to reflect this month of May on Mary, the beloved mother of our Lord, the holy spouse of the Holy Spirit, and the role of the Holy Spirit in shaping the destiny of our Catholic Church.

We knew recently that the two Supreme Pontiffs of the Church had been canonized who are great advocates in promoting the Holy Spirit in the heart of the spiritual life of the Church. Besides, all their encyclicals had been concluded always seeking the intercession of our Lady full of grace who interceded miraculously during the wedding feast in Cana in Galilee.

Let me reflect now on: The Blessed Virgin Mary: "Immaculate Spouse of the Holy Spirit"

The month of May is cordially dedicated in honor of our Lady which in my home country, Philippines, we call it "Flores de Mayo." What a joy to know that here in our parish of Sacred Heart we pray with affection the mysteries of the Holy Rosary everyday and even before Mass.

We have in fact a lovely "Living Rosary" and it is Scriptural and offering roses and rain of rose petals. The root word for Rosary is rose, one of the titles of our Lady is "Mystical Rose." By praying the Rosary, we are not only meditating the mystery of the life of Jesus and the Blessed Mother but we are offering our loving devotion by offering spiritual bouquet of roses to heaven where our Lady is crowned as Queen of all angels and saints.

During the 'dormition' which is the deep sleep of our Lady, and based on the tradition of the Church, St. Thomas the Apostle was searching for our Lady and when he opened the door where our Lady was resting, the apostle found nothing except the "bed of roses."

Indeed, it was affirmed by the roses of Tepeyac, Mexico that St. Juan Diego brought the roses during untimely season of flowers during winter December 12 to the Bishop for him to believe and the "tilma" where the roses were placed, became the most miraculous icon of our Lady of Guadalupe.

Today scientists continue to marvel at the unfathomable miracle which happened during the middle ages and even today. This is because the Holy Spirit is guiding our holy Mother Church. In human language I would say that Mary is the Immaculate Spouse of the Holy Spirit in the sense that in our profession of faith we say: "She conceived by the Holy Spirit." Our Lady conceived Jesus, the second person of the Most Holy Trinity by the Holy Spirit. Hence, Mary is the Immaculate Spouse of the Holy Spirit.

It was the archangel St. Gabriel from the synoptic gospels that he announced that the virgin will conceive by the Holy Spirit. Our Lady was not blind obedient to the angel, she verified by asking: "How can this be since I am a virgin?" And the angel replied: "The power of the Most High will over shadow you and you will bear a son conceived by the Holy Spirit.

At Pentecost, the Holy Spirit in the form of tongues of fire descends upon Mary and upon the holy apostles at the Upper room in Jerusalem after 50 days of the resurrection of our Lord Jesus Christ.

The Church is a sleeping giant if there is no Pentecost. St. Pope John the XXIII opened the portal of the Church to its Pentecost experience, the Second Vatican Council and which brings forth renewal "aggiornamento" to the universal Church.

And in his loving memory perpetuated by his successors especially by St. John Paul II, the Great whom he recognized the great role of the Holy Spirit in the very life of the Church. The Holy Spirit then is the very soul of the Church who sanctify us and making as saints.

Without the Holy Spirit, the Church is indeed likened to a "sleeping giant." But because of the Holy Spirit the priesthood of all the baptized had been recognized and empowered.

Their special role in the various ministries had been invigorated and they became vibrant agents of sanctification. It is the same Holy Spirit then whom we received in baptism who is operative in our lives. His charisms poured out upon us and His gifts in Confirmation had been bestowed upon us, whom we are sealed for our redemption.

On the other hand, the Immaculate Spouse of the Holy Spirit, the Blessed Virgin Mary which the Church recognises today as the Star of the New Evangelization. Who else is closer to the Holy Spirit? I would say: Mary, our blessed mother and "the immaculate spouse of the Holy Spirit."

In our parish pastoral ministry and in the springtime of the life of our parish, I humbly commend all our efforts, discernment, pastoral planning, our goals, our journey, hopes and dreams to the intercession of Our Lady that she may intercede before her son, Jesus.

May the Holy Spirit will make His dwelling among us so that all of us will be renewed by His transforming love, be aided by supernatural grace necessary for building up God's kingdom and our parish will be as dynamic as the early Church refreshed by the Pentecost.

May the Holy Spirit continue to strengthen us with His unfailing help as we are preparing for the birthday of the Church, the Pentecost Sunday and on our days of preparations for the success of Life in the Spirit holy retreat in honor of the Holy Spirit Himself, the Advocate and our Comforter.

As your shepherd, I highly encourage you to actively participate in the out pouring of the Holy Spirit during our Life in the Spirit retreat, a unique encounter with the Risen Lord whose Spirit abides with us until the end of the world. Rest assured of my prayers that the grace whom you received in Baptism and in Confirmation will be stirred by the warmth of the fire of love that comes from the Holy Spirit himself. The those whose faith is lukewarm will be renewed, on fire, and alive again.

Let us open our hearts, let the door of our Church be open wide to the Holy Spirit whom Mary welcomed and she became the ark of the new covenant. Come Holy Spirit and renew our parish and the entire strata of humanity and of the whole world. Amen

St. Joseph the Worker: ***"Patron of our Archdiocese of Edmonton, of our country, Canada and of the entire Universal Church, Pray for us!"***

Let us imitate the heroic virtues of Saint Joseph, upright and righteous man of Galilee. As head of the Holy Family of Nazareth, we can learn about practical arts of daily Christian living from him. Though he was so silent, it seemed never spoke in the gospels but only being described by the evangelists.

Thus, I can tell that St. Joseph is indeed the very model of contemplative life. Always attuned to the voice of God, he listened more to the one who has the words of eternal life.

St Joseph's best known virtues are surely his humility, his openness to God's plan, his ready and perfect obedience, his silence, and his loving care for Jesus and Mary. He is now revered as the patron of the universal Church, a title that was officially recognized in 1847 by Blessed Pius IX.

Today, we might focus on the great number of saints who have nurtured devotion to the great Patriarch of the faith, Joseph of Nazareth. However, there is another aspect of devotion to St Joseph that is often overlooked now a days. He is the patron of a happy death. Sensitive souls meditating on Joseph had made the happy supposition that he died in the arms of Jesus and Mary and so had the best possible death.

In the Gospels the figure of the foster father fades away after the episode of the finding of Jesus in the temple. Nevertheless, his name is still spoken of when the people - amazed by the teaching and miracles of Jesus – ask, "Is this not the carpenter's son? But Joseph himself no longer appears.

Tradition has it that he died having completed his vocation to act as father to the Son of God on earth. Joseph must have left this world by the time Jesus reached maturity, as it would be difficult to explain his absence when Jesus began his ministry or why he was not there at the foot of the cross on Calvary.

His death came while he was enveloped in the love of those two most perfect hearts: the Sacred Heart of Jesus whom our parish church and catholic school were named after, and the Immaculate Heart of Mary.

For Christians, no better death is imaginable than one at which Jesus and Mary are present. Their great love accompanied Joseph in the last and most difficult part of this life. Of course in past times (and even today) it was considered desirable to die at home in one's own bed. More than that, our faith makes us long for the consoling love of Jesus and Mary when we die. This thought prompted the prayer to St Joseph asking for the grace to die in circumstances similar to his.

To meditate on the life of St. Joseph, we are made whole and consoled again that through his intercession we are not alone and feeling depressed because he is our patron on our earthly sojourn and also patron interceding before his foster son, our Lord Jesus

Christ in the hour of our death. Likewise to our Lady too as we often say, pray for us sinners now and at the hour of our death. Amen

May through the solemn intercession of St. Joseph, the most chaste spouse of the Blessed Virgin Mary, we may meet our Lord Jesus Christ at the end of our earthly journey as we request also the intercession of our Lady praying, "show unto us the blessed fruit of your womb, Jesus". May the Most Sacred Heart of Jesus be no longer our judge at our particular judgment but as "Merciful Saviour".

Let us welcome the beautiful icon of the patron of our Archdiocese with utmost respect and prayerful reverence. We are blessed of his visitation in our three Churches and catholic school especially this month of May which is the month of his feast.

Let us pray devoutly the prayer printed in a prayer card as a gift for each one of you, dear young friends in the Sacred Heart Catholic School of Wetaskiwin. Let us pray often and invoke God's blessings for our bright future through the intercession of our patriarch, St. Joseph. With my prayerful best wishes to all of you friends....

Printed by
Schaltungsdienst Lange o.H.G., Berlin